Books by this author:

The Whore and her Mother
9/11, Babylon and the return of the king

Oh What Rapture!
Arrows bible prophecy series, book #1

Is a 'secret rapture' going to spare believers from tribulation to come?

Neighbours from Hell
Arrows bible prophecy series, book #2

Israel and the coming nuclear attempt to destroy her

Facing the Beast
Arrows bible prophecy series, book #3

The man they call the antichrist and our response to him

In Six Hours ... the world changed

Apocalyptic fiction thriller

In One Hour ... Babylon will fall

Apocalyptic fiction thriller – sequel

Ireland – now the good news!
The best of *'Bread'* – personal testimonies and church/fellowship profiles from around Ireland

Edited by *Raymond & Gerry McCullough*

A Wee Taste a' Craic

all the Irish craic from the *Celtic Roots Radio* shows, 2-25

Cover design: Raymond McCullough

Cover photos: Burning city © Fotorince Dreamstime.com
Adult man in suit © Gcammarata I Dreamstime.com

Facing the Beast

Raymond McCullough

Comments on The Whore and her Mother:

"... AMAZED when I read this book ... in awe of your extensive knowledge on so many levels: Christian, Jewish, and Muslim culture; the Jewish diaspora ... Greek & Hebrew; and your panoramic view of history through a biblical world view ... thought-provoking and troublesome ... many will be offended, but you consistently build your case instead of being sensationalistic."
      James Revoir, author of *Priceless Stones*

"... thoughtful, insightful ... and you have a knack for putting complicated topics in an easily accessible way."
      Jim Darcy, author of *The Firelord's Crown*

".. has the makings of a best seller in its field ... you open up real ideas some of which are somewhat scary to say the least ... difficult to leave down because you have created the 'Must turn the page' feeling threaded right through every line"
      Colin T Mercer, UK, author & poet

"Love this kind of stuff ... grounded in research and common sense"
      Francis Albert McGrath, Dublin, Ireland, author

"... most thought provoking ... meticulously researched and written with style and passion"
      Sheila Belshaw, UK, author of *Pinpoint*

"It's very thought-provoking and solidly presented."
      Katherine Holmes, author of *The Swan Bonnet*

"I did not feel you were preaching at all, more laying your cards on the table ... An evocative read, which left me 'thoughtful'"
      Molly Hopkins, author of *It Happened in Paris*

"I was so impressed with the level of detail you give and your breadth of knowledge ... well-researched and thorough"
      Kevin Alex Baker, author of *Head Games*

Facing the Beast

The man they call the antichrist and our response to him

Raymond McCullough

Published by

Copyright © Raymond McCullough, 2020

The right of **Raymond McCullough** to be identified as author of this work has been asserted by him in accordance with the **Copyright, Design and Patents Act, 1988**

ISBN 13: 978-0-9955404 6 0

ISBN 10: 0-9955404 6 2

First published **2020**

All rights reserved.

No part of this publication may be reproduced or transmitted in any form or by any means, electronic or mechanical, including photocopy, recording, or any information storage and retrieval system, without permission in writing from the publisher.

THE HOLY BIBLE, NEW INTERNATIONAL VERSION®, NIVUK®

Copyright © 1973, 1978, 1984, 2011 by Biblica, Inc.™

Used by permission. All rights reserved worldwide.

10a Listooder Road, Crossgar, Downpatrick, Northern Ireland BT30 9JE

Contents

Introduction	1
1 – Who is the beast?	3
2 – Beasts and empires	10
3 – King of the North	22
4 – Gog, of the land of Magog	32
5 – Woman and ten-horned beast	42
6 – The destroyer of Babylon	52
7 – The beast is revealed	62
8 – The mark of the beast	74
9 – The Great Tribulation	84
10 – The mother of all battles	98
11 – The end of the Beast	106
12 – Millennium reign of Messiah	116
13 – Facing the Beast	126
Bibliography	145
Appendix	146
About the author:	148

Thanks to my wife, Gerry, for editing and general encouragement

Introduction

Several years ago, after publishing my first bible prophecy book, *'The Whore and her Mother,'* a close friend gave me a prophetic word. He shared a picture he had of me firing arrows. I believe it was a *word of wisdom* directing me to focus on one prophetic topic at a time – targeting it, as it were. Thus the *'Arrows bible prophecy series'* was birthed.

So far there are three books in the series: *'Oh What Rapture!,' 'Neighbours from Hell'* and *'Facing the Beast.'* This third book in the series deals with the beast of Revelation, who was prophesied about long before in the Tanakh (Old Testament).

He is known by several names, or titles, and – although the *'spirit of antichrist'* has been at work in the world since New Testament times (**1 John 2:18-23**) – he is currently being hindered from being revealed (**2 Thessalonians 2:6,7**), but when that hindrance is removed then he will be revealed to the world.

He will *'make war'* against Jews/Israelites and Christian believers (Revelation 13:5-8), persecuting them without mercy – and will rule over all the nations of the earth.

- Who is he?
- When will he be revealed?
- How will he come to power?
- The destroyer of Babylon
- How will he rule?
- How long will he reign?
- How will he be defeated?
- How can we survive his rule?

Facing the Beast – *Raymond McCullough*

He is known throughout the prophets under several different titles:

- The Beast: **Revelation 11:7**
- The Antichrist: **1 John 2:22**
- The Man of Sin: **2 Thessalonians 2:3**
- The Lawless One: **2 Thessalonians 2:8**
- The Little Horn: **Daniel 7:8**
- The prince that will come: **Daniel 9:26**
- The vile person: **Daniel 11:21**
- The willful king: **Daniel 11:36**
- The profane and wicked prince: **Ezekiel 21:25**
- Gog, of the land of Magog: **Ezekiel 38**

1 – Who is the beast?

The bible – both old and new testament – refer to a man who will come to power in the last days. Many different descriptions are used – the antichrist, the beast, the man of sin, the prince who will come.

Yeshua – Jesus – warned his early disciples, *'Watch out that no one deceives you. For many will come in my name, claiming, "I am the Messiah," and will deceive many.'* (**Matthew 24:4.5**) The antichrist – the name means anti-Messiah, against the messiah, or in place of the messiah – will appear as a saviour to the whole world. *'The whole world was filled with wonder and followed the beast.'* (**Revelation 13:3**)

Although Yeshua did not refer directly to this man, he *did* refer to his actions:

> **Matthew 24:15** 'So when you see standing in the holy place "the abomination that causes desolation," spoken of through the prophet Daniel – let the reader understand – 16 then let those who are in Judea flee to the mountains.

Yeshua expected that his disciples would be there to see this event. Many believers – especially in the USA – are putting their trust in a false prophecy of a *'secret rapture'*, where they hope to be rescued and caught up to heaven so as to avoid any confrontation with this man. When Yeshua returns, we will certainly be caught up to meet him, but it will be no secret!

The first book in this series – *Oh what Rapture!* – looked at this subject in depth and exposed this unbiblical lie. Few believers in China, the Middle East, or in other countries where persecution is common, believe this nonsense. Remember Yeshua's first words on the subject were, *'Watch out that no one deceives you.'* He also warned us that *'in this world you will have trouble'* (**John 16:33**) – in fact he said:

> **Matthew 24:9** 'Then you will be handed over to be persecuted and put to death, and you will be hated by all nations

because of me. 10 <u>At that time many will turn away from the faith and will betray and hate each other</u>, 11 and many false prophets will appear and deceive many people. 12 Because of the increase of wickedness, <u>the love of most will grow cold</u>, 13 but the one who stands firm to the end will be saved. 14 And this gospel of the kingdom will be preached in the whole world as a testimony to all nations, <u>and then the end will come.</u>

Not only will many be deceived, but the result of that deception and subsequent disillusionment will be that *'they will turn away from the faith, betray and hate each other'* – *'the love of most will grow cold.'* The apostle Paul warned of this time to come – i.e. the time of Jesus' return *'and our being gathered to him':*

2 Thessalonians 2 The man of lawlessness

2 <u>Concerning the coming of our Lord Jesus Christ and our being gathered to him</u>, we ask you, brothers and sisters, 2 not to become easily unsettled or alarmed by the teaching allegedly from us – whether by a prophecy or by word of mouth or by letter – asserting that the day of the Lord has already come. 3 <u>Don't let anyone deceive you in any way, for that day will not come until the rebellion occurs and the man of lawlessness is revealed</u>, the man doomed to destruction. 4 He will oppose and will exalt himself over everything that is called God or is worshipped, so that he sets himself up in God's temple, proclaiming himself to be God.

Paul gives us some new information about this *'man of lawlessness'* – literally *'man opposed to the Torah,'* God's law. So, he is against God's law, against the Messiah and, as we shall see, against God's people – both Jews and Christian believers. He will actually proclaim himself to *be* God.

Paul says the day of our being gathered to him (Yeshua) will NOT come until the rebellion occurs and until the *'man of lawlessness'* is revealed. What is the rebellion Paul refers to? Other translations put this as *'the apostasy'*, or *'falling away from the faith'* – exactly what Yeshua said in Matthew 24. So, not surprisingly, Paul and Yeshua are saying the same thing.

Paul tells us two more facts in the verses above – the man of lawlessness *'will oppose and will exalt himself over*

Chapter 1 – Who is the beast?

everything that is called God or is worshipped, so that he sets himself up in God's temple, proclaiming himself to be God.'

Yeshua referred to *'an abomination that causes desolation … standing in the holy place.'* We understand now from Paul that the holy place is the temple of God – i.e. the Jewish temple in Jerusalem. But that temple has yet to be built, so this cannot happen straight away. So, does this mean that Jesus cannot return *'at any moment'* – exactly! Now you are getting the picture. In fact, *several* events must take place before Yeshua's return.

The fourth fact that Paul gives us is that the man of lawlessness is *'doomed to destruction.'* Well, that is good news! Paul adds some detail to this in verse 8:

2 Thessalonians 2:8 Then that lawless one will be revealed whom the Lord will slay with the breath of His mouth and bring to an end by the appearance of His coming.

The man of lawlessness will be brought to an end by the appearance of Yeshua – his second coming. He *'will slay* [the beast] *with the breath of His mouth.'* So where do we get the phrase *'the beast'* from?

Both the prophet Daniel and the apostle John, in Revelation, tell us about a future empire and its leader, collectively known as the beast:

Revelation 13:13 The dragon stood on the shore of the sea. And I saw a beast coming out of the sea. It had ten horns and seven heads, with ten crowns on its horns, and on each head a blasphemous name. 2 The beast I saw resembled a leopard, but had feet like those of a bear and a mouth like that of a lion. The dragon gave the beast his power and his throne and great authority. 3 One of the heads of the beast seemed to have had a fatal wound, but the fatal wound had been healed. The whole world was filled with wonder and followed the beast. 4 People worshipped the dragon because he had given authority to the beast, and they also worshipped the beast and asked, 'Who is like the beast? Who can wage war against it?'

5 The beast was given a mouth to utter proud words and blasphemies and to exercise its authority for forty-two months. 6 It opened its mouth to blaspheme God, and to slander his

name and his dwelling-place and those who live in heaven. 7 <u>It was given power to wage war against God's holy people and to conquer them</u>. And it was given authority over every tribe, people, language and nation. 8 All inhabitants of the earth will worship the beast – all whose names have not been written in the Lamb's book of life, the Lamb who was slain from the creation of the world. 9 Whoever has ears, let them hear. 10 'If anyone is to go into captivity, into captivity they will go. If anyone is to be killed with the sword, with the sword they will be killed.' This calls for patient endurance and faithfulness on the part of God's people.

This beast is quite fantastical in its description – it resembles a leopard, but has feet like a bear and a mouth like a lion. On top of this it has seven heads and ten horns! We might recognise this animal if we ever saw it, right? But we *won't* ever see this – this is a prophetic vision, similar to those given to Daniel in the Tanakh. Each part of the description is symbolic and we need to understand what the symbols mean.

Firstly, the dragon who *'gave the beast his power and his throne and great authority'* is a reference to the devil – Satan, the adversary:

Revelation 12:9 And the great dragon was thrown down, the serpent of old who is called the devil and Satan, who deceives the whole world.

Secondly, the beast comes out of the sea:

Daniel 7:2 Daniel said, "I was looking in my vision by night, and behold, the four winds of heaven were <u>stirring up the great sea</u>. 3 And four great beasts were <u>coming up from the sea</u>, different from one another.

16 I approached one of those who were standing by and began asking him the exact meaning of all this. So he told me and made known to me the interpretation of these things: 17 '<u>These great beasts</u>, which are four in number, <u>are four kings who will arise from the earth</u>.

So the beasts of Daniel 7 are kings, who arise from the earth. The sea represents the nations of the world. The antichrist will arise out of the nations of the world. Let's skip

Chapter 1 – Who is the beast?

the heads and horns – which we will look at in due course. The next fact to note about this man is that:

> **Revelation 13:5** <u>The beast was given a mouth to utter proud words and blasphemies</u> and to exercise its authority for <u>forty-two months</u>. 6 <u>It opened its mouth to blaspheme God</u>, and to slander his name and his dwelling-place and those who live in heaven. 7 <u>It was given power to wage war against God's holy people and to conquer them</u>. ... 10 <u>This calls for patient endurance and faithfulness</u> on the part of God's people.

He will *'wage war against God's holy people and ... conquer them.'* But he has a limited time – only 3½ years – to rule. This is confirmed in both Daniel and Revelation:

> **Daniel 7:25** <u>He will speak out against the Most High and wear down the saints of the Highest One</u>, and he will intend to make alterations in times and in law; <u>and they will be given into his hand for a time, times, and half a time</u>.

> **Daniel 12:7** I heard the man dressed in linen, who was above the waters of the river, as he raised his right hand and his left toward heaven, and swore by Him who lives forever that <u>it would be for a time, times, and half a time; and as soon as they finish shattering the power of the holy people, all these events will be completed</u>.

> **Revelation 12:14** But the two wings of the great eagle were given to the woman, so that she could fly into the wilderness to her place, where <u>she was nourished for a time and times and half a time, from the presence of the serpent</u>.

Not only is he the antichrist, but he is opposed to anything Christian (or Jewish). The reference in all three cases is to years – a year, two years and half a year – again 3½ years. The woman also represents *'the holy people'*, but we will look at that later. So, we have four confirmations that his rule over the people of God will only last 3½ years.

> **Revelation 13:7** And <u>it was given authority over every tribe, people, language and nation. 8 All inhabitants of the earth will worship the beast</u> – all whose names have not been written in the Lamb's book of life, the Lamb who was slain from the creation of the world.

This is total world domination – some people think the beast will only rule over his own kingdom, but this verse makes it clear – '*authority over every tribe, people, language and nation.*' The antichrist will rule over the whole world – a one world government.

Chapter 1 – Who is the beast?

Who is the beast?

1. Jesus warned his early disciples, *'Watch out that no one deceives you.'* The antichrist will fool the whole world. We need to be wary of false teachings. (**Matthew 24:4**) Paul also says, *'Don't let anyone deceive you.'* (**2 Thessalonians 2:3**)

2. Yeshua did not refer directly to this man, but *did* refer to his actions – *'the abomination of desolation … standing in the holy place,'* i.e. the Jewish temple. (**Matthew 24:15**)

3. Deception will cause many to *'turn away from the faith, betray and hate each other,' 'the love of most will grow cold.'* (**Matthew 24:10,12; 2 Thessalonians 2:3**)

4. The beast is a *'man of lawlessness'* – i.e. opposed to God's law, the Torah. (**2 Thessalonians 2:3**)

5. He will *'set himself up in God's temple, proclaiming himself to be God'* – the *'abomination of desolation'* spoken of by both Yeshua and Daniel. (**2 Thessalonians 2:4; Matthew 24:15; Daniel 7:25, 11:36**)

6. He is *'doomed to destruction'*, Yeshua *'will slay* [him] *with the breath of His mouth.'* (**2 Thessalonians 2:3,8**)

7. The great dragon who *'gave the beast his power and his throne and great authority'* is the devil, Satan. (**Revelation 12:9, 13:1,2,4**)

8. The beast rises from the sea, just like the four beasts in Daniel's vision – the sea being the nations of the earth. (**Revelation 13:1; Daniel 7:1-3**)

9. He will *'make war'* on *'the holy people of God,' 'wear down the saints of the Highest One.'* (**Daniel 7:25, 12:7; Revelation 13:5**)

10. He has a limited time to achieve this – only 3½ years. (**Daniel 7:25, 12:7; Revelation 12:14, 13:5**)

11. He *'was given authority over every tribe, people, language and nation. All inhabitants of the earth will worship the beast.'* (**Revelation 13:3,4,7**)

2 – Beasts and empires

The beast in Revelation 13 has seven heads, which, we will discover represent seven different empires. To verify this we need to look some more at the prophet Daniel, who not only had his own dream of the four beasts, but interpreted a previous dream of Nebuchadnezzar, king of Babylon – where Daniel had been taken as a captive. He and his friends had been trained in Babylonian ways and learning and served in the king's palace. (**Daniel 1:1-7**)

Daniel 2:2 In the second year of his reign, Nebuchadnezzar had dreams; his mind was troubled and he could not sleep. 2 So the king summoned the magicians, enchanters, sorcerers and astrologers to tell him what he had dreamed. When they came in and stood before the king, 3 he said to them, 'I have had a dream that troubles me and I want to know what it means.'

4 Then the astrologers answered the king, 'May the king live for ever! Tell your servants the dream, and we will interpret it.'

5 The king replied to the astrologers, 'This is what I have firmly decided: if you do not tell me what my dream was and interpret it, I will have you cut into pieces and your houses turn ed into piles of rubble. 6 But if you tell me the dream and explain it, you will receive from me gifts and rewards and great honour. So tell me the dream and interpret it for me.'

7 Once more they replied, 'Let the king tell his servants the dream, and we will interpret it.'

8 Then the king answered, 'I am certain that you are trying to gain time, because you realise that this is what I have firmly decided: 9 if you do not tell me the dream, there is only one penalty for you. You have conspired to tell me misleading and wicked things, hoping the situation will change. So then, tell me the dream, and I will know that you can interpret it for me.'

10 The astrologers answered the king, 'There is no one on earth who can do what the king asks! No king, however great and mighty, has ever asked such a thing of any magician or

enchanter or astrologer. 11 What the king asks is too difficult. No one can reveal it to the king except the gods, and they do not live among humans.'

12 This made the king so angry and furious that he ordered the execution of all the wise men of Babylon. 13 So the decree was issued to put the wise men to death, and men were sent to look for Daniel and his friends to put them to death.

14 When Arioch, the commander of the king's guard, had gone out to put to death the wise men of Babylon, Daniel spoke to him with wisdom and tact. 15 He asked the king's officer, 'Why did the king issue such a harsh decree?' Arioch then explained the matter to Daniel. 16 At this, Daniel went in to the king and asked for time, so that he might interpret the dream for him.

17 Then Daniel returned to his house and explained the matter to his friends Hananiah, Mishael and Azariah. 18 He urged them to plead for mercy from the God of heaven concerning this mystery, so that he and his friends might not be executed with the rest of the wise men of Babylon. 19 During the night the mystery was revealed to Daniel in a vision. Then Daniel praised the God of heaven 20 and said:

'Praise be to the name of God for ever and ever; wisdom and power are his. 21 He changes times and seasons; he deposes kings and raises up others. He gives wisdom to the wise and knowledge to the discerning. 22 He reveals deep and hidden things; he knows what lies in darkness, and light dwells with him. 23 I thank and praise you, God of my ancestors: you have given me wisdom and power, you have made known to me what we asked of you, you have made known to us the dream of the king.'

Daniel interprets the dream

24 Then Daniel went to Arioch, whom the king had appointed to execute the wise men of Babylon, and said to him, 'Do not execute the wise men of Babylon. Take me to the king, and I will interpret his dream for him.' 25 Arioch took Daniel to the king at once and said, 'I have found a man among the exiles from Judah who can tell the king what his dream means.'

26 The king asked Daniel (also called Belteshazzar), 'Are you able to tell me what I saw in my dream and interpret it?'

27 Daniel replied, 'No wise man, enchanter, magician or diviner can explain to the king the mystery he has asked about,

Chapter 2 – Beasts and empires

<u>28 but there is a God in heaven who reveals mysteries. He has shown King Nebuchadnezzar what will happen in days to come</u>. Your dream and the visions that passed through your mind as you were lying in bed are these:

29 'As Your Majesty was lying there, your mind turned to things to come, and the revealer of mysteries showed you what is going to happen. 30 As for me, this mystery has been revealed to me, not because I have greater wisdom than anyone else alive, but so that Your Majesty may know the interpretation and that you may understand what went through your mind.

31 'Your Majesty looked, and there before you stood a large statue – an enormous, dazzling statue, awesome in appearance. 32 The head of the statue was made of pure gold, its chest and arms of silver, its belly and thighs of bronze, 33 its legs of iron, its feet partly of iron and partly of baked clay. 34 While you were watching, a rock was cut out, but not by human hands. It struck the statue on its feet of iron and clay and smashed them. 35 Then the iron, the clay, the bronze, the silver and the gold were all broken to pieces and became like chaff on a threshing-floor in the summer. The wind swept them away without leaving a trace. But the rock that struck the statue became a huge mountain and filled the whole earth.

36 'This was the dream, and now we will interpret it to the king. 37 Your Majesty, you are the king of kings. The God of heaven has given you dominion and power and might and glory; 38 in your hands he has placed all mankind and the beasts of the field and the birds in the sky. Wherever they live, he has made you ruler over them all. You are that head of gold.

39 'After you, another kingdom will arise, inferior to yours. Next, a third kingdom, one of bronze, will rule over the whole earth. 40 Finally, there will be a fourth kingdom, strong as iron – for iron breaks and smashes everything – and as iron breaks things to pieces, so it will crush and break all the others. 41 Just as you saw that the feet and toes were partly of baked clay and partly of iron, so this will be a divided kingdom; yet it will have some of the strength of iron in it, even as you saw iron mixed with clay. 42 As the toes were partly iron and partly clay, so this kingdom will be partly strong and partly brittle. 43 And just as you saw the

iron mixed with baked clay, so the people will be a mixture and will not remain united, any more than iron mixes with clay.

44 'In the time of those kings, the God of heaven will set up a kingdom that will never be destroyed, nor will it be left to another people. It will crush all those kingdoms and bring them to an end, but it will itself endure for ever. 45 This is the meaning of the vision of the rock cut out of a mountain, but not by human hands – a rock that broke the iron, the bronze, the clay, the silver and the gold to pieces.

'The great God has shown the king what will take place in the future. The dream is true and its interpretation is trustworthy.'

46 Then King Nebuchadnezzar fell prostrate before Daniel and paid him honour and ordered that an offering and incense be presented to him. 47 The king said to Daniel, 'Surely your God is the God of gods and the Lord of kings and a revealer of mysteries, for you were able to reveal this mystery.'

48 Then the king placed Daniel in a high position and lavished many gifts on him. He made him ruler over the entire province of Babylon and placed him in charge of all its wise men. 49 Moreover, at Daniel's request the king appointed Shadrach, Meshach and Abednego chief ministers over the province of Babylon, while Daniel himself remained at the royal court.

Daniel and his friends first heard of this dream of the king when they were told they were about to be executed – along with all the wise men of Babylon. A desperate situation – so Daniel asked the king for time to interpret the dream. Then he and his Jewish friends prayed to *'the God of heaven'* and God answered by giving Daniel a *'vision in the night.'* He also gave Daniel understanding of what the dream meant.

The statue was made of gold, silver, bronze, iron and clay, and Daniel told the king that he, Nebuchadnezzar, was the head of gold – i.e. the Babylonian empire. The chest and arms of silver represented the empire to come after the Babylonian – i.e. the Medo-Persian empire. The belly and thighs of bronze represented the Greek empire, and the iron legs the Roman empire.

We know that the Roman empire was divided into two – east and west – the eastern empire of Byzantium lasting longer

Chapter 2 – Beasts and empires

then the west, which was overcome by the Visigoths, Vandals, Huns and Franks. However, the vision of the feet and toes – partly of iron and partly of baked clay (a strange and unusual mixture, which we will come back to later) – referred to the latter days of this empire.

The great metal statue

- head of pure gold = **Babylon**
- chest and arms of silver = **Medo-Persia**
- belly and thighs of bronze = **Greece**
- legs of iron = **Rome** (and Byzantium)
- feet partly of iron, partly of baked clay = final empire

The empire statue was destroyed by the kingdom of God, which smashed the statue into pieces *'without leaving a trace'* and the kingdom of God *'filled the whole earth'* in its place. The rock struck the statue on its feet of iron and clay – so the kingdom of God will appear at the time when the toes of iron and clay are in control – a time still to come.

Daniel survived the fall of ancient Babylon and served also under the Medo-Persian rulers. He had several other revelations and dreams concerning the coming empires of Persia and Greece, which we will look at in due course. Let's now look at his own dream of the four beasts:

> **Daniel 7:1** In the first year of Belshazzar king of Babylon, Daniel had a dream, and visions passed through his mind as he was lying in bed. He wrote down the substance of his dream. 2 Daniel said: 'In my vision at night I looked, and there before me were the four winds of heaven churning up the great sea. 3 <u>Four great beasts, each different from the others, came up out of the sea</u>.
>
> 4 '<u>The first was like a lion, and it had the wings of an eagle</u>. I watched until its wings were torn off and it was lifted from the ground so that it stood on two feet like a human being, and the mind of a human was given to it. 5 '<u>And there before me was a second beast, which looked like a bear</u>. It was raised up on one of its sides, and it had

three ribs in its mouth between its teeth. It was told, "Get up and eat your fill of flesh!"

6 'After that, I looked, and there before me was <u>another beast, one that looked like a leopard</u>. And on its back it had four wings like those of a bird. This beast had four heads, and it was given authority to rule.

'After that, in my vision at night I looked, <u>and there before me was a fourth beast – terrifying and frightening and very powerful</u>. It had large iron teeth; it crushed and devoured its victims and trampled underfoot whatever was left. <u>It was different from all the former beasts, and it had ten horns</u>.

8 'While I was thinking about the horns, <u>there before me was another horn, a little one, which came up among them; and three of the first horns were uprooted before it. This horn had eyes like the eyes of a human being and a mouth that spoke boastfully</u>.

Still in the midst of his vision, Daniel approaches an angel and asks for the meaning of all this:

> **Daniel 7:15** 'I, Daniel, was troubled in spirit, and the visions that passed through my mind disturbed me. 16 I approached one of those standing there and asked him the meaning of all this.
>
> '<u>So he told me and gave me the interpretation of these things</u>: 17 "<u>The four great beasts are four kings that will rise from the earth</u>. 18 But the holy people of the Most High will receive the kingdom and will possess it for ever – yes, for ever and ever."

This is very much in parallel to the king's dream of the metal statue. The beasts represent four kingdoms – empires – and *'the holy people of the Most High will receive the kingdom and will possess it for ever.'* The outcome is the same – the beasts of empire will be taken over by the kingdom of God.

Daniel's dream refers to four great beasts, which came out of the sea – just like the one beast in John's vision in Revelation. Daniel is told that these are four kings that will rise from the earth – not just kings, but empires. In Daniel's earlier interpretation of king Nebuchadnezzar's dream of a metal statue (Daniel 2), it represented the Babylonian, Medo-

Chapter 2 – Beasts and empires

Persian, Greek and Roman Empires – plus another later one, which had similarities with the Roman. The beasts here represent these same empires – the fourth beast, the Roman Empire, being the one with ten horns, plus the *'little horn'*.

> **Daniel 7:19** 'Then I wanted to know the meaning of the fourth beast, which was different from all the others and most terrifying, with its iron teeth and bronze claws – the beast that crushed and devoured its victims and trampled underfoot whatever was left. 20 <u>I also wanted to know about the ten horns on its head and about the other horn that came up, before which three of them fell</u> – **the horn that looked more imposing than the others and that had eyes and a mouth that spoke boastfully.** <u>21 As I watched, this horn was waging war against the holy people and defeating them, 22 until the Ancient of Days came</u> and pronounced judgment in favour of the holy people of the Most High, and the time came when they possessed the kingdom.
>
> 23 'He gave me this explanation: "The fourth beast is a fourth kingdom that will appear on earth. It will be <u>different from all the other kingdoms</u> and will devour the whole earth, trampling it down and crushing it. 24 <u>The ten horns are ten kings who will come from this kingdom. After them another king will arise, different from the earlier ones; he will subdue three kings. 25 He will speak against the Most High and oppress his holy people and try to change the set times and the laws. The holy people will be delivered into his hands for a time, times and half a time</u>.
>
> 26 '"But the court will sit, and his power will be taken away and completely destroyed for ever. 27 Then <u>the sovereignty, power and greatness of all the kingdoms under heaven will be handed over to the holy people of the Most High</u>. His kingdom will be an everlasting kingdom, and all rulers will worship and obey him."
>
> 28 'This is the end of the matter. I, Daniel, was deeply troubled by my thoughts, and my face turned pale, but I kept the matter to myself.'

The four beasts out of the sea

- a lion with wings of an eagle = **Babylon**
- a bear with three ribs in its mouth = **Medo-Persia**
- a leopard with four wings = **Greece**
- a terrifying beast with large iron teeth = **Rome**
- the little horn = ruler of final empire
- the kingdom of God

The *'fourth kingdom ... will be different from all the other kingdoms and will devour the whole earth.'* Ten kings will come from this kingdom, then another king will arise *'different from the earlier ones'* and will *'subdue three kings'*. Then comes the clue to who this king is, i.e. *'the little horn'*:

> **Daniel 7:25** <u>He will speak against the Most High and oppress his holy people</u> and try to change the set times and the laws. <u>The holy people will be delivered into his hands for a time, times and half a time</u>.

We are talking about the antichrist here. He has not yet appeared and neither have the ten kings, represented by the other ten horns. Now we are not just talking about an empire, but the ruler – the *'little horn'* – who controls that empire. This man is *'more imposing than the others'* (the other ten rulers) arrogant – he had *'eyes and a mouth that spoke boastfully'*. *'He will speak against the Most High and oppress his holy people.'* Who are *'his holy people'* – Jews, Israelites and bible believing Christians.

Daniel uses some other titles for this person. We have already seen the reference in Daniel 7 to the *'little horn'*. In chapter 8 Daniel has another vision, this time of a ram with two horns, being charged by a goat with a single horn and trampled by it – more beasts, in other words! The ram represented the kings of Media and Persia and the shaggy goat the Greek empire of Alexander the Great. The single horn was broken off and replaced by four horns – the four smaller kingdoms into which the Greek empire was divided following the death of Alexander – ruled by his commanders.

Chapter 2 – Beasts and empires

Daniel 8:8 The goat became very great, but at the height of its power the large horn was broken off, and in its place four prominent horns grew up towards the four winds of heaven.

9 Out of one of them came another horn, which started small but grew in power to the south and to the east and towards the Beautiful Land. 10 It grew until it reached the host of the heavens, and it threw some of the starry host down to the earth and trampled on them. 11 It set itself up to be as great as the commander of the army of YHWH; it took away the daily sacrifice from YHWH, and his sanctuary was thrown down. 12 Because of rebellion, YHWH's people and the daily sacrifice were given over to it. It prospered in everything it did, and truth was thrown to the ground.

This vision begins as a prophecy about the Medo-Persian Empire being overcome by the future Greek Empire of Alexander and the four separate kingdoms that emerged from that empire. But the prophecy suddenly jumps forward to the end times, describing the antichrist, who *'took away the daily sacrifice from YHWH.'* The angel, Gabriel, is told to explain the vision to Daniel:

Daniel 8:15 While I, Daniel, was watching the vision and trying to understand it, there before me stood one who looked like a man. 16 And I heard a man's voice from the Ulai calling, 'Gabriel, tell this man the meaning of the vision.'

17 As he came near the place where I was standing, I was terrified and fell prostrate. 'Son of man,' he said to me, 'understand that the vision concerns the time of the end.' 18 While he was speaking to me, I was in a deep sleep, with my face to the ground. Then he touched me and raised me to my feet.

19 He said: 'I am going to tell you what will happen later in the time of wrath, because the vision concerns the appointed time of the end. 20 The two-horned ram that you saw represents the kings of Media and Persia. 21 The shaggy goat is the king of Greece, and the large horn between its eyes is the first king. 22 The four horns that replaced the one that was broken off represent four

kingdoms that will emerge from his nation but will not have the same power.

23 'In the latter part of their reign, when rebels have become completely wicked, <u>a fierce-looking king, a master of intrigue, will arise. 24 He will become very strong, but not by his own power. He will cause astounding devastation and will succeed in whatever he does. He will destroy those who are mighty, the holy people. 25 He will cause deceit to prosper, and he will consider himself superior. When they feel secure, he will destroy many and take his stand against the Prince of princes. Yet he will be destroyed, but not by human power</u>.

26 'The vision of the evenings and mornings that has been given you is true, but seal up the vision, for it concerns the distant future.'

We learn from this that *'the vision concerns the time of the end'* and *'what will happen later in the time of wrath, because the vision concerns the appointed time of the end.'* The *'time of wrath'* will occur at the very end of the last days. *'In the latter part of their reign, when rebels have become completely wicked'* this king will arise. Daniel is told to *'seal up the vision, for it concerns the distant future.'* In other words, none of this has happened yet.

What can we learn about this king – *'another horn, which started small but grew in power'* – who fits the previous descriptions of the antichrist to a T? Notice one thing here – beasts and heads represent empires, but horns represent individual kings. This *'little horn'* is fierce looking, a master of intrigue. '*He will become very strong, but <u>not by his own power</u>.*' Compare this with the descriptions of Paul and John:

2 Thessalonians 2:9 <u>The coming of the lawless one will be in accordance with how Satan works. He will use all sorts of displays of power through signs and wonders</u> that serve the lie, 10 and all the ways that wickedness deceives those who are perishing.

Revelation 13:2 <u>The dragon gave the beast his power</u> and his throne and great authority.

Chapter 2 – Beasts and empires

> **Daniel 8:24** He will cause astounding devastation and will succeed in whatever he does. 25 He will cause deceit to prosper, and he will consider himself superior.

> **Daniel 8:12** It prospered in everything it did, and truth was thrown to the ground

Compare these verses with John's description of his ability and arrogance:

> **Revelation 13:4** People worshipped the dragon because he had given authority to the beast, and they also worshipped the beast and asked, 'Who is like the beast? Who can wage war against it?' 5 The beast was given a mouth to utter proud words and blasphemies

> **Daniel 8:11** It set itself up to be as great as the commander of the army of YHWH.

'The little horn' will be very arrogant, but also very powerful – speaking proud words, using lying and deceit to further his ambitions – *'truth was thrown to the ground.'*

'The little horn' also *'started small but grew in power to the south and to the east and towards the Beautiful Land* [Israel].' So, to determine the little horn's origin we should look north and west of Israel – but still within the Seleucid Empire (northern successors to Alexander) – to find the origin of this king. Turkey is looking very likely, isn't it?

Notice that the prophetic incidences of a beast, or beasts, always refer to empires so a point to note is that:

beast = empire

The heads are also described as mountains (Revelation 17:9) which, in the prophetic word, again refers to empires.

The beast (from Daniel 7 and Revelation 13) has ten horns – plus *'the little horn'* – so:

a horn = an individual king

Beasts and empires – summary:

1. Nebuchadnezzar had a dream of a metallic statue, which represented at least four empires – Babylon, Medo-Persia, Greece and Rome. (**Daniel 2:1-49**)

2. The worldly empire statue was smashed in pieces and replaced by the kingdom of God – the rock specifically hit the feet of iron and clay. (**Daniel 2:34-35,44-45**)

3. Daniel's own dream was of four beasts, who came out of the sea – nations of the world. Again we have the four empires already mentioned. **beast = empire**. (**Daniel 7:1-28**)

4. The fourth beast had ten horns, which were ten kings – **a horn = an individual king** (**Daniel 7:7,19-20,23-24**)

5. In addition another *'little horn'* arises – the antichrist. (**Daniel 7:20-21,24-25**)

6. Like the statue in Nebuchadnezzar's dream the beast empires come to an end – *'the holy people of the Most High will receive the kingdom and will possess it for ever.'* (**Daniel 7:18**)

7. His rise to power will be by the power of Satan – *'The dragon gave the beast his power and his throne and great authority'* (**Revelation 13:2**) and *'the coming of the lawless one will be in accordance with how Satan works.'* (**2 Thessalonians 2:9**)

8. He will be proud, arrogant and deceitful – he *'was given a mouth to utter proud words'* (**Revelation 13:5**) and *'truth was thrown to the ground.'* (**Daniel 8:12**)

9. He will come from somewhere to the north and west of Israel, but still within the former Seleucid (Greek) Empire – *'started small but grew in power to the south and to the east and towards the Beautiful Land* [Israel].' (**Daniel 8:9**)

10. **beast/head = empire** and **horn = individual king**

3 – King of the North

Again, in chapters 10 and 11, Daniel is given more revelation, referring to the coming Greek Empire which, as we said above, became divided into four kingdoms – north, south, east and west – after the death of Alexander.

> **Daniel 11:2** 'Now then, I tell you the truth: three more kings will arise in Persia, and then a fourth, who will be far richer than all the others. When he has gained power by his wealth, he will stir up everyone against the kingdom of Greece. 3 Then a mighty king will arise [Alexander, the great], who will rule with great power and do as he pleases. 4 After he has arisen, his empire will be broken up and parcelled out towards the four winds of heaven. It will not go to his descendants, nor will it have the power he exercised, because his empire will be uprooted and given to others.

The remainder of this prophecy refers to a number of conflicts between the *'king of the north'* (i.e. the Seleucid kingdom of Turkey/Syria/Iraq) and the *'king of the south'* (the kingdom of Egypt, ruled by the Ptolemy dynasty). The prophecy gives great detail of a period of history that have become known as the Syrian Wars – from 260-169 BCE.

> **Daniel 11:31** 'His armed forces will rise up to desecrate the temple fortress and will abolish the daily sacrifice. Then they will set up the abomination that causes desolation. 32 With flattery he will corrupt those who have violated the covenant, but the people who know their God will firmly resist him.
>
> 33 'Those who are wise will instruct many, though for a time they will fall by the sword or be burned or captured or plundered. 34 When they fall, they will receive a little help, and many who are not sincere will join them. 35 Some of the wise will stumble, so that they may be refined, purified and made spotless until the time of the end, for it will still come at the appointed time.

The last *'king of the north'* mentioned (**Daniel 11:21-32**) refers in part to the Seleucid king, Antiochus IV Ephiphanes, who erected a statue of Zeus in the Jewish Temple in Jerusalem – this was the original *'abomination of desolation'*. However, this is not the complete fulfilment of this prophecy because, long after Antiochus IV's time it is referred to by Yeshua, himself:

> **Matthew 24:14** And this gospel of the kingdom will be preached in the whole world as a testimony to all nations, <u>and then the end will come</u>.
>
> 15 '<u>So when you see standing in the holy place "the abomination that causes desolation," spoken of through the prophet Daniel – let the reader understand – 16 then let those who are in Judea flee to the mountains.</u> 17 Let no one on the housetop go down to take anything out of the house. 18 Let no one in the field go back to get their cloak. 19 How dreadful it will be in those days for pregnant women and nursing mothers! 20 Pray that your flight will not take place in winter or on the Sabbath. 21 For then there will be great distress, unequalled from the beginning of the world until now – and never to be equalled again.

So, according to Yeshua's own words, this prophecy has yet another fulfilment, still to be seen. The actions of Antiochus in 177/8 BCE – setting up a statue of Zeus in the Temple – were a *type* of another event yet to come which refers specifically to the antichrist. Again, he is described as using flattery (deceit) to *'corrupt those who have violated the covenant.'*

From chapter 11 verse 21 on Daniel's prophecy does not relate to any events that have been fulfilled in the past, but refers to the future – only the beast *'will exalt and magnify himself above every god and will say unheard-of things against the God of gods':*

> **Daniel 11:36** 'The king will do as he pleases. <u>He will exalt and magnify himself above every god and will say unheard-of things against the God of gods.</u>

So, let's now look at this prophecy of Daniel, step by step:

> **Daniel 11:21** 'He will be succeeded by <u>a contemptible person</u> who has not been given the honour of royalty. <u>He will invade the kingdom [Israel] when its people feel secure, and he will</u>

Chapter 3 – King of the North

seize it through intrigue. 22 Then an overwhelming army [of Israel] will be swept away before him; both it and a prince of the covenant will be destroyed.

At some point this *'king of the north'* will invade Israel – *'when its people feel secure,'* defeating their army and killing an Israeli leader. This has a parallel with a ruler described in a prophecy of Ezekiel:

> **Ezekiel 38:8** In future years you will invade a land that has recovered from war, whose people were gathered from many nations to the mountains of Israel, which had long been desolate. They had been brought out from the nations, and now all of them live in safety.
>
> 10 you will devise an evil scheme. 11 You will say, 'I will invade a land of unwalled villages; I will attack a peaceful and unsuspecting people – all of them living without walls and without gates and bars.

This is certainly not describing Israel's situation today – no way could present-day Israel be described as *'feeling secure'*, or *'peaceful and unsuspecting'*. (See my previous book, *Neighbours from Hell*, for more on this)

> 23 After coming to an agreement with him, he will act deceitfully, and with only a few people he will rise to power.

This describes an agreement (covenant) made with Israel which the king then breaks (just like Hitler's agreement with Stalin in WWII). Again this has a parallel with Daniel's *'Seventy Weeks'* prophecy, which also describes an agreement being broken and Israel being invaded:

> **Daniel 9:26** The people of the ruler who will come will destroy the city and the sanctuary. The end will come like a flood: war will continue until the end, and desolations have been decreed. 27 He will confirm a covenant with many for one 'seven.' In the middle of the 'seven' he will put an end to sacrifice and offering. And at the temple he will set up an abomination that causes desolation, until the end that is decreed is poured out on him.

The *'king of the north'* and the *'ruler who will come'* are the same person – the beast – who will make this agreement/covenant, which he will then break at his convenience

– leading to an invasion of Israel, the sacrifices being ended and the abomination being set up.

> **Daniel 11:24** <u>When the richest provinces feel secure, he will invade them</u> and will achieve what neither his fathers nor his forefathers did. <u>He will distribute plunder, loot and wealth among his followers</u>. He will plot the overthrow of fortresses – but only for a time.

He will come to take plunder – again we have parallels with Ezekiel's prophecy:

> **Ezekiel 38:12** <u>I will plunder and loot</u> and turn my hand against the resettled ruins and the people gathered from the nations, <u>rich in livestock and goods</u>, living at the centre of the land [earth].' 13 Sheba and Dedan and the merchants of Tarshish and all her villages will say to you, '<u>Have you come to plunder? Have you gathered your hordes to loot, to carry off silver and gold, to take away livestock and goods and to seize much plunder?</u>'"

The next few verses seem to repeat what we have already seen – his war with the *'king of the south,'* who will be betrayed, will lead him to turn against Israel and the 'holy covenant' – leading to the invasion, removal of sacrifices and the abomination being set up.:

> **Daniel 11:25** 'With a large army he will stir up his strength and courage against the king of the South. The king of the South will wage war with a large and very powerful army, but he will not be able to stand because of the plots devised against him. 26 Those who eat from the king's provisions will try to destroy him; his army will be swept away, and many will fall in battle. 27 The two kings, <u>with their hearts bent on evil, will sit at the same table and lie to each other,</u> but to no avail, because an end will still come at the appointed time. 28 The king of the North will return to his own country <u>with great wealth, but his heart will be set against the holy covenant. He will take action against it and then return to his own country.</u>
>
> 29 '<u>At the appointed time</u> he will invade the South again, but this time the outcome will be different from what it was before. 30 Ships of the western coastlands will oppose him, and he will lose heart. Then <u>he will turn back and vent his fury</u>

Chapter 3 – King of the North

against the holy covenant. He will return and show favour to those who forsake the holy covenant.

31 'His armed forces will rise up to desecrate the temple fortress and will abolish the daily sacrifice. Then they will set up the abomination that causes desolation..

The *'king of the south'* in the earlier parts of this prophecy referred to the Greek Ptolemaic kingdom of Egypt, which also included Libya and Sudan. The *'king of the north'* is frustrated and turns his attention to Israel and is especially vehement *'against the holy covenant'*. This is when he will set up the *'abomination that causes desolation'* and *'will abolish the daily sacrifice.'* As we read above in Daniel 9, *'in the middle of the 'seven' he will put an end to sacrifice and offering.'*

Daniel 11:32 With flattery he will corrupt those who have violated the covenant, but the people who know their God will firmly resist him. 33 'Those who are wise will instruct many, though for a time they will fall by the sword or be burned or captured or plundered. 34 When they fall, they will receive a little help, and many who are not sincere will join them. 35 Some of the wise will stumble, so that they may be refined, purified and made spotless until the time of the end, for it will still come at the appointed time.

36 'The king will do as he pleases. He will exalt and magnify himself above every god and will say unheard-of things against the God of gods. He will be successful until **the time of wrath** is completed, for what has been determined must take place. 37 He will show no regard for the gods of his ancestors or for the one desired by women, nor will he regard any god, but will exalt himself above them all. 38 Instead of them, he will honour a god of fortresses; a god unknown to his ancestors he will honour with gold and silver, with precious stones and costly gifts. 39 He will attack the mightiest fortresses with the help of a foreign god and will greatly honour those who acknowledge him. He will make them rulers over many people and will distribute the land at a price.

The apostle Paul refers to this also:

2 Thessalonians 2:3-4 That day will not come until the rebellion occurs and the man of lawlessness is revealed, the man doomed to destruction. 4 He will oppose and will exalt himself over everything that is called God or is worshipped,

<u>so that he sets himself up in God's temple, proclaiming himself to be God</u>.

The only end-time ruler who fits this description is the anti-christ. Some prophecy writers have suggested that the beast will be Islamic – perhaps the long-awaited Islamic *Mahdi*, which may well be true – but it is obvious here that this king only regards <u>himself</u> as God. He really is a true servant of Satan.

When he abolishes the daily sacrifice he will then begin his crusade against believers and *'those who are wise will instruct many, though for a time they will fall by the sword or be burned or captured or plundered'*. This will be a time for believers to stand out as witnesses to the true God, though the price may well be their lives. As Yeshua said, *'If they persecuted me, they will persecute you'* (**John 15:20**) and *'you will be handed over to be persecuted and put to death, and you will be hated by all nations because of me.'* (**Matthew 24:8-9**)

> 40 '<u>At the time of the end</u> the king of the South will engage him in battle, and the king of the North will storm out against him with chariots and cavalry and a great fleet of ships. He will invade many countries and sweep through them like a flood. 41 <u>He will also invade the Beautiful Land</u>. Many countries will fall, <u>but Edom, Moab and the leaders of Ammon will be delivered from his hand</u>.

Note: *'he will invade the beautiful land'* [Israel] – *'but Edom, Moab and the leaders of Ammon will be delivered from his hand.'* In Matthew 24 Yeshua warns those in Judaea and Jerusalem to flee to the mountains when they *'see the abomination of desolation standing in the holy place.'*

Edom, Moab and Ammon are no longer nations by this time – they correspond to today's Kingdom of Jordan – but their territory has already been taken over by Israel in the *Six Hour War* of Psalm 83, Isaiah 17, etc. (Book #2 of this series – *Neighbours from Hell* – covers those events). So, are the people of Jerusalem and Judea meant to flee to the mountains of Moab, Ammon and Edom – present-day Jordan?

Many students of prophecy believe that Petra and the mountains there are intended to be a safe refuge for Israel in

Chapter 3 – King of the North

those days. That could well be – certainly John refers to *'a place prepared for her in the wilderness':*

> **Revelation 12:13** When the dragon saw that he had been hurled to the earth, he pursued the woman [Israel] who had given birth to the male child [Yeshua]. 14 <u>The woman was given the two wings of a great eagle, so that she might fly to the place prepared for her in the wilderness, where she would be taken care of for a time, times and half a time, out of the snake's reach</u>. 15 Then from his mouth the snake spewed water like a river, to overtake the woman and sweep her away with the torrent. 16 <u>But the earth helped the woman by opening its mouth and swallowing the river that the dragon had spewed out of his mouth</u>. 17 Then the dragon was enraged at the woman and went off to wage war against the rest of her offspring – those who keep God's commands and hold fast their testimony about Jesus.

> **Daniel 11:42** <u>He will extend his power over many countries;</u> Egypt will not escape. 43 He will gain control of the treasures of gold and silver and all the riches of Egypt, with the Libyans and Cushites in submission. 44 But reports from the east and the north will alarm him, and <u>he will set out in a great rage to destroy and annihilate many. 45 He will pitch his royal tents between the seas at the beautiful holy mountain</u>. Yet he will come to his end, and no one will help him.

The antichrist will eventually return to Israel, bringing all the nations of the world against her – assembling the armies at a pace called Har Megiddo (Armageddon – a flat area in northern Israel) in order to attack and destroy Jerusalem. That's when God himself will intervene!

> **Daniel 12:1** *'*<u>At that time Michael</u>, the great prince who protects your people, <u>will arise. There will be a time of distress such as has not happened from the beginning of nations until then</u>.

In Hebrew prophecy the phrase, *'at that time'*, is always taken to refer to the end times. This is further confirmed by the references to *'the time of the end'* (v.40) and *'the time of wrath.'* (v.36) This *'time of distress'* is different from the *'time of Jacob's trouble'* and the *'Great Tribulation.'* This will be the pouring out of God's wrath on the nations and God's people *will* be delivered from it – by being raised from the dead or, if still living, *'caught up'* to meet the Lord in the air.

Daniel 12:1 But <u>at that time</u> your people – everyone whose name is found written in the book – will be delivered. 2 <u>Multitudes who sleep in the dust of the earth will awake: some to everlasting life, others to shame and everlasting contempt.</u> 3 Those who are wise will shine like the brightness of the heavens, and those who lead many to righteousness, like the stars for ever and ever.

'Multitudes who sleep in the dust of the earth will awake: some to everlasting life.' This is the first resurrection. John refers to this also:

Revelation 20:4 They came to life and reigned with Christ for a thousand years. 5 (The rest of the dead did not come to life until the thousand years were ended.) <u>This is the first resurrection. 6 Blessed and holy are those who share in the first resurrection</u>. The second death has no power over them, but they will be priests of God and of Christ and will reign with him for a thousand years.

There *is* a second resurrection – the resurrection to judgement, which John tells us is not *'until the thousand years [have] ended,'* or as Daniel puts it a resurrection *'to shame and everlasting contempt.'*

King of the north – summary:

1. **Daniel 11:1-4** predicts the rise of a great king – Alexander – and the breaking up of his empire after his death *'towards the four winds of heaven.'*

2. The following sixteen verses predict what became known as the Syrian Wars – from 260-169 BCE – between two former parts of the Greek empire – the kings of the north and the kings of the south, i.e. the Seleucid and Ptolemaic kingdoms.

3. From verse 21 on, though, the prophecies have yet to be fulfilled and the *'king of the north'* described corresponds with many things we already know of the antichrist.

4. Verse 31 describes how he will *'abolish the daily sacrifice'* and *'will set up the abomination that causes desolation.'* These are the actions of the antichrist.

5. Although Antiochus IV did set up a statue of Zeus, desecrating the Jewish Temple (167 BC) – a partial fulfilment of v.31, i.e. a *type* of what is to come – according to Yeshua's own words in **Matthew 24**, this prophecy has yet to be fulfilled.

6. *'He will be a contemptible person who ... will invade the kingdom* [Israel] *when its people feel secure.'* This compares with Ezekiel's prophecy of a ruler who *'will attack a peaceful and unsuspecting people.'* (**Ezekiel 38:8-11**)

7. This invasion will take place after making an agreement with the Israeli leader (*'prince of the covenant'*), deceitfully breaking the agreement and killing the prince – also referred to in the *Seventy Weeks* prophecy in **Daniel 9:27**: *'He will confirm a covenant with many for one 'seven.' In the middle of the 'seven' he will put an end to sacrifice and offering.'*

8. He will come to take plunder (**Daniel 11:24**) – also in **Ezekiel 38:12-13**: *'silver and gold ... livestock and goods.'*

9. *'He will exalt and magnify himself above every god and will say unheard-of things against the God of gods.'* (**v.36**) – see also **2 Thessalonians 2:4**.

10. He will commence persecuting believers – *'those who are wise ... for a time will fall by the sword or be burned or captured or plundered'* – as Yeshua said, *'If they persecuted me, they will persecute you'* (**John 15:20**) and *'you will be hated by all nations because of me.'* (**Matthew 24:8-9**)

11. Although he *'will invade the Beautiful Land,'* *'Edom, Moab and the leaders of Ammon will be delivered from his hand'* – but Edom, Moab and Ammon (Jordan) will be part of Israel by this time, so will this mean Israelis can escape to safety in former Jordan – it seems likely and fits with Yeshua's warning to *'flee to the mountains'* in **Matthew 24** and John's reference to the woman [Israel] having a *'place prepared for her in the wilderness.'* (**Revelation 12:14**)

12. Eventually *'in great rage'* he will bring all his armies into Israel (**v.45**) to attack Jerusalem – then he will come to an end!

13. *'There will be a time of distress such as has not happened from the beginning of nations until then,'* in other words the outpouring of God's wrath upon the nations.

14. *'At that time'* God's people – *'everyone whose name is found written in the book'* – will be delivered! This is the first resurrection (**Revelation 20:4-5**) *'Multitudes who sleep in the dust of the earth will awake: some to everlasting life.'* (**Daniel 12:1-3**) Those who *'are alive and remain'* will be *'caught up to meet the Lord in the air.'* (**1 Thessalonians 4:13-18**)

4 – Gog, of the land of Magog

There is another prophecy which we should now consider – often treated as a separate event in the prophetic calendar, but there are so many parallels with what we have already covered – and that is Ezekiel's *'Gog and Magog'* prophecy in chapters 38 and 39. Before we look at it in detail let's first jump to verse 17:

> **Ezekiel 38:17** "'This is what the Sovereign YHWH says: <u>you are the one I spoke of in former days by my servants the prophets of Israel. At that time they prophesied for years that I would bring you against them</u>.

So, where else is there a prophecy about Gog and Magog? Well – apart from the (much later) book of Revelation – there isn't one! So to what is YHWH referring in this verse? Other prophets have spoken of this person that Ezekiel calls Gog – *'they prophesied for years that I would bring you* [Gog] *against them* [Israel].*'* So, if Gog is not mentioned, who were these prophets speaking about? Well, the *'prince that will come'*, the *'king of the north'*, the *'little horn'* are all mentioned – in other words, the beast, the antichrist. There are no other prophecies that fit, so Ezekiel must also here be referring to the antichrist.

Micah is the first prophet to mention anyone coming against Israel:

> **Micah 1:15** <u>I will bring a conqueror against you</u> who live in Mareshah.

(Mareshah sounds like the Hebrew word for *'conqueror'*.)

> **Ezekiel 38:1** The word of YHWH came to me: 2 'Son of man, set your face against <u>Gog</u>, of the land of Magog, <u>the chief prince</u> of Meshek and Tubal; prophesy against him 3 and say: "This is what the Sovereign YHWH says: I am against you, Gog, chief prince of Meshek and Tubal. 4 I will turn you around, put hooks in your jaws and bring you out with your whole army – your horses, your horsemen fully armed, and a great horde

with large and small shields, all of them brandishing their swords. 5 Persia, Cush and Put will be with them, all with shields and helmets, 6 also Gomer with all its troops, and Beth Togarmah from the far north with all its troops – <u>the many nations with you</u>.

7 "'Get ready; be prepared, <u>you and all the hordes gathered about you, and take command of them</u>. 8 <u>After many days</u> you will be called to arms. <u>In future years you will invade a land that has recovered from war, whose people were gathered from many nations to the mountains of Israel</u>, which had long been desolate. They had been brought out from the nations, <u>and now all of them live in safety</u>. 9 You and all your troops and the many nations with <u>you will go up, advancing like a storm; you will be like a cloud covering the land</u>.

Gog is a ruler – *'of the land of Magog'* (a son of Japheth, along with his brothers, Gomer, Meshek and Tubal – **Genesis 10:2**). He is *'the chief prince of Meshek and Tubal'* – *'Persia* [Iran], *Cush* [Ethiopia] *and Put* [Libya] *will be with them ... also Gomer with all its troops, and Beth Togarmah* [son of Gomer] *from the far north with all its troops – the many nations with you.'*

This is getting to be pretty fair-sized coalition. We have nine biblical nations represented plus *'the many nations with you'* – this could be maybe twenty nations or perhaps a lot more. Certainly a huge army – verse 7 says, *'all the hordes gathered about you.'* Could this really be a separate event from the armies of the antichrist gathering for Arnageddon? I don't think so.

Where are these nations today? Can we identify them? We are told (verse 6) that Beth Togarmah is *'from the far north'* and verse 15 tells us that *'You* [Gog] *will come from your place in the far north.'* But before you jump to any conclusions let's remember that *'the far north'* is a phrase being used by a Hebrew prophet who prophesied shortly after the time Israel were taken into captivity in Babylon – i.e. around 594 BC. He lived in Tel Aviv – no, not the city in Israel! – he lived in an area of Babylon called Tel Aviv!

The tribes he mentions are regarded by most scholars as living at that time in the area of Asia Minor – in other

Chapter 4 – Gog, of the land of Magog

words, modern day Turkey. From the perspective of someone taken captive from Israel the *'far north'* would have been in what is now Turkey. This dovetails with what we learned earlier about the *'king of the north'* who came from somewhere north and west of Israel, but still within the Greek Seleucid (Syrian) empire, which included the area that is now known as Turkey.

> **Ezekiel 38:10** "'This is what the Sovereign YHWH says: on that day thoughts will come into your mind and you will devise an evil scheme. 11 You will say, 'I will invade a land of unwalled villages; <u>I will attack a peaceful and unsuspecting people – all of them living without walls and without gates and bars. 12 I will plunder and loot and turn my hand against the resettled ruins and the people gathered from the nations, rich in livestock and goods, living at the centre of the land [earth]</u>.' 13 Sheba and Dedan and the merchants of Tarshish and all her villages will say to you, 'Have you come to plunder? Have you gathered your hordes to loot, to carry off silver and gold, to take away livestock and goods and to seize much plunder?'"

Israel is *'a peaceful and unsuspecting people – all of them living without walls and without gates and bars'* living in *'the resettled ruins and ... gathered from the nations,'* – because this takes place after the *Six Hour War* (**Psalm 83**, etc.), where all the surrounding nations – *'malicious neighbours'* (**Ezekiel 28:24**) – have been defeated and exiled (see my previous book, *'Neighbours from Hell'* for details of this war).

This antichrist invasion of Israel and removal of the sacrifices is also described in the book of Joel:

> **Joel 1:6** <u>A nation has invaded my land, a mighty army without number; it has the teeth of a lion, the fangs of a lioness</u>. 7 It has laid waste my vines and ruined my fig-trees. It has stripped off their bark and thrown it away, leaving their branches white. 8 Mourn like a virgin in sackcloth grieving for the betrothed of her youth. 9 <u>Grain offerings and drink offerings are cut off from the house of YHWH</u>. The priests are in mourning, those who minister before YHWH.
>
> 13 Put on sackcloth, you priests, and mourn; wail, you who minister before the altar. Come, spend the night in sackcloth, you who minister before my God; for <u>the grain offerings and drink offerings are withheld from the house of your God</u>.

14 Declare a holy fast; call a sacred assembly. Summon the elders and all who live in the land to the house of YHWH your God, and cry out to YHWH. 15 <u>Alas for that day! For the day of YHWH is near; it will come like destruction from the Almighty</u>.

Ezekiel 38:14 'Therefore, son of man, prophesy and say to Gog: "This is what the Sovereign YHWH says: <u>in that day, when my people Israel are living in safety</u>, will you not take notice of it? 15 <u>You will come from your place in the far north, you and many nations with you</u>, all of them riding on horses, a great horde, a mighty army. 16 <u>You will advance against my people Israel like a cloud that covers the land</u>. In days to come, Gog, <u>I will bring you against my land</u>, so that the nations may know me when I am proved holy through you before their eyes.

17 '"This is what the Sovereign YHWH says: <u>you are the one I spoke of in former days by my servants the prophets of Israel. At that time they prophesied for years that I would bring you against them</u>. 18 This is what will happen in that day: when Gog attacks the land of Israel, <u>my hot anger will be aroused</u>, declares the Sovereign YHWH.

YHWH is aroused to hot anger – does not bode well for Gog and all his armies.

Ezekiel 38:19 In my zeal and fiery wrath <u>I declare that at that time there shall be a great earthquake in the land of Israel</u>. 20 The fish in the sea, the birds in the sky, the beasts of the field, every creature that moves along the ground, and <u>all the people on the face of the earth will tremble</u> at my presence. <u>The mountains will be overturned, the cliffs will crumble and every wall will fall to the ground</u>.

This great earthquake – which will overturn mountains – is also mentioned by the apostle John, who says, *'every mountain and island was removed from its place':*

Revelation 6:12 I watched as he opened the sixth seal. <u>There was a great earthquake</u>. The sun turned black like sackcloth made of goat hair, the whole moon turned blood red, 13 and the stars in the sky fell to earth, as figs drop from a fig-tree when shaken by a strong wind. 14 The heavens receded like a scroll being rolled up, and <u>every mountain and island was removed from its place</u>. 15 Then the kings of the earth, the princes, the generals, the rich, the mighty, and everyone

Chapter 4 – Gog, of the land of Magog

else, both slave and free, hid in caves and among the rocks of the mountains. 16 They called to the mountains and the rocks, 'Fall on us and hide us from the face of him who sits on the throne and from the wrath of the Lamb! 17 For the great day of their wrath has come, and who can withstand it?'

In Ezekiel YHWH says, *'all the people on the face of the earth will tremble at my presence'* and in Revelation *'everyone else, both slave and free, hid in caves and among the rocks of the mountains. They called to the mountains and the rocks, 'Fall on us and hide us from the face of him who sits on the throne.'*

> **Ezekiel 38:21** I will summon a sword against Gog on all my mountains, declares the Sovereign YHWH. Every man's sword will be against his brother. 22 I will execute judgment on him with plague and bloodshed; I will pour down torrents of rain, hailstones and burning sulphur on him and on his troops and on the many nations with him. 23 And so I will show my greatness and my holiness, and I will make myself known in the sight of many nations. Then they will know that I am YHWH."

The destruction of these great armies will occur in two ways – *'every man's sword will be against his brother,'* but also YHWH himself will intervene *'with plague and bloodshed; I will pour down torrents of rain, hailstones and burning sulphur on him and on his troops and on the many nations with him.'* This sounds very similar to what happened to Sodom, Gomorrah and the other towns of the Jordan valley:

> **Genesis 19:24** Then YHWH rained down burning sulphur on Sodom and Gomorrah – from YHWH out of the heavens. 25 Thus he overthrew those cities and the entire plain, destroying all those living in the cities.

The destruction of these armies is also described by the prophet Zechariah:

> **Zechariah 14:12** This is the plague with which YHWH will strike all the nations that fought against Jerusalem: their flesh will rot while they are still standing on their feet, their eyes will rot in their sockets, and their tongues will rot in their mouths. 13 On that day people will be stricken by YHWH with great panic. They will seize each other by the hand and attack one another. 14 Judah too will fight at Jerusalem. The wealth

of all the surrounding nations will be collected – great quantities of gold and silver and clothing. 15 A similar plague will strike the horses and mules, the camels and donkeys, and all the animals in those camps.

Again the destruction is twofold – they will fight against one another and also YHWH will strike them by his own hand with something resembling a nuclear devastation. Ezekiel continues the story in chapter 39:

> **Ezekiel 39:1** 'Son of man, prophesy against Gog and say: "This is what the Sovereign YHWH says: I am against you, Gog, chief prince of Meshek and Tubal. 2 I will turn you around and drag you along. I will bring you from the far north and send you against the mountains of Israel. 3 Then I will strike your bow from your left hand and make your arrows drop from your right hand. 4 <u>On the mountains of Israel you will fall</u>, you and all your troops and the nations with you. <u>I will give you as food to all kinds of carrion birds and to the wild animals. 5 You will fall in the open field</u>, for I have spoken, declares the Sovereign YHWH. 6 <u>I will send fire on Magog and on those who live in safety in the coastlands</u>, and they will know that I am YHWH.
>
> 17 'Son of man, this is what the Sovereign YHWH says: <u>call out to every kind of bird and all the wild animals</u>: "Assemble and <u>come together from all around to the sacrifice I am preparing for you, the great sacrifice on the mountains of Israel. There you will eat flesh and drink blood</u>. 18 You will eat the flesh of mighty men and drink the blood of the princes of the earth as if they were rams and lambs, goats and bulls – all of them fattened animals from Bashan. 19 At the sacrifice I am preparing for you, <u>you will eat fat till you are glutted and drink blood till you are drunk. 20 At my table you will eat your fill of horses and riders, mighty men and soldiers of every kind</u>," declares the Sovereign YHWH.

Gog's armies will fall on the mountains of Israel – they will never reach Jerusalem, but will become a feast for *'carrion birds and … wild animals.'* Again this has a parallel in Revelation:

> **Revelation 19:17** And I saw an angel standing in the sun, who <u>cried in a loud voice to all the birds flying in mid-air, 'Come, gather together for the great supper of God, 18 so that you may eat the flesh of kings, generals, and the mighty, of horses

Chapter 4 – Gog, of the land of Magog

<u>and their riders, and the flesh of all people, free and slave, great and small</u>.'

19 Then I saw <u>the beast and the kings of the earth and their armies gathered together</u> to wage war against the rider on the horse [Yeshua] and his army. 20 But the beast was captured, and with it the false prophet who had performed the signs on its behalf. With these signs he had deluded those who had received the mark of the beast and worshipped its image. The two of them were thrown alive into the fiery lake of burning sulphur. 21 The rest were killed with the sword coming out of the mouth of the rider on the horse, and <u>all the birds gorged themselves on their flesh</u>.

The beast, and all the kings and armies who followed him to attack and destroy Israel, will be completely wiped out on the mountains of Israel.

Ezekiel 39:7 "'I will make known my holy name among my people Israel. I will no longer let my holy name be profaned, and the nations will know that I YHWH am the Holy One in Israel. 8 It is coming! It will surely take place, declares the Sovereign YHWH. <u>This is the day I have spoken of.</u>

All through the scriptures the prophets speak of the coming *Day of YHWH* – the *Day of the Lord*.

9 "'Then those who live in the towns of Israel will go out and use the weapons for fuel and burn them up – the small and large shields, the bows and arrows, the war clubs and spears. For seven years they will use them for fuel. 10 They will not need to gather wood from the fields or cut it from the forests, because they will use the weapons for fuel. And they will plunder those who plundered them and loot those who looted them, declares the Sovereign YHWH.

11 "'<u>On that day I will give Gog a burial place in Israel, in the valley of those who travel east of the Sea</u>. It will block the way of travellers, because <u>Gog and all his hordes will be buried there</u>. So it will be called the Valley of Hamon Gog.

12 "'For seven months the Israelites will be burying them in order to cleanse the land. 13 All the people of the land will bury them, and the day I display my glory will be a memorable day for them, declares the Sovereign YHWH. 14 People will be continually employed in cleansing the land. They will spread

out across the land and, along with others, they will bury any bodies that are lying on the ground.

"'After the seven months they will carry out a more detailed search. 15 As they go through the land, anyone who sees a human bone will leave a marker beside it until the gravediggers bury it in the Valley of Hamon Gog, 16 near a town called Hamonah. And so they will cleanse the land.''

Chapter 4 – Gog, of the land of Magog

Gog, of the land of Magog – summary:

1. YHWH says, *'you are the one I spoke of in former days by my servants the prophets of Israel'* (**Ezekiel 38:17**) No other prophet in the Tanakh spoke of Gog, or the land of Magog, but they do speak of the beast under other titles – so Gog is another name for the antichrist.

2. Micah was the earliest prophet to speak of this man: *'I will bring a conqueror against you.'* (**Micah 1:15**)

3. Gog is the ruler *'of the land of Magog'* and *'the chief prince* of *Meshek and Tubal'*. Gomer and Beth Togarmah are with him. Magog was a son of Japheth, along with his brothers, Gomer, Meshek and Tubal; Togarmah was the son of Gomer; so all these tribes are related (**Genesis 10:2**) and were reckoned by scholars to live in the area of Asia Minor in Ezekiel's time – i.e. modern-day Turkey.

4. They are joined by Persia [Iran], Cush [Ethiopia] and Put [Libya] and *'the many nations with you.'* This is a huge coalition of armies – hard to differentiate this from the antichrist, who will bring *'all nations'* against Israel –

'I will gather all the nations to Jerusalem to fight against it'. (**Zechariah 14:2**)

5. Both Gog and Beth Togarmah are described as *'from the far north'*, though this has to be seen from the perspective of Ezekiel, recently exiled from Israel to Babylon, so Asia Minor could easily be spoken of as *'the far north'*.

6. Asia Minor fits with the *'king of the north'* who comes from north and west of Israel – again modern day Turkey.

7. He invades *'a peaceful and unsuspecting people ... living without walls gates* [or] *bars'* in *'the resettled ruins ... gathered from the nations,'* – i.e. after the *Six Hour War* (**Psalm 83**, etc.). All their *'malicious neighbours'* are long gone. (**Ezekiel 28:24**) – see *'Neighbours from Hell'*.

8. *'A mighty army without number has invaded my land,'* and *'offerings are cut off from the house of YHWH.'* (**Joel 1:6,9,13**, **Ezekiel 28:24**)

9. YHWH is aroused to *'hot anger'* and *'there will be a great earthquake in the land of Israel.* (**Ezekiel 38:19**) Also in **Revelation 6:12** – *'mountains will be overturned* and *'islands removed from* [their] *place.'*

10. YHWH says, *'all the people on the face of the earth will tremble at my presence'* (**Ezekiel 38:20**) and *'everyone else ... called to the mountains and the rocks, 'Fall on us and hide us from the face of him who sits on the throne."* (**Revelation 6:16**)

11. YHWH says, *'I will pour down rain, hailstones and burning sulphur on him ... and the many nations with him,'* (**Ezekiel 38:22**) – just like he did to Sodom and Gomorrah. (**Genesis 19:24**) This *'plague'* is also described by the prophet Zechariah. (**Zechariah 14:12-14**)

12. *'On the mountains of Israel you will fall, you and all ... the nations with you,'* (**Ezekiel 39:4**) and the armies will become a feast for carrion birds and wild animals. (**Ezekiel 39:4-20**) Again prophesied in **Revelation 19:17-21**.

13. This is the *Day of YHWH* – the *Day of the Lord* – spoken about by many of the prophets.

14. It will take Israel seven months to bury the bodies of the fallen armies of the beast and for seven years they will use the discarded weapons for fuel – plus *'great quantities of gold and silver and clothing.'*

5 – Woman and ten-horned beast

Revelation 17:3 Then the angel carried me away in the Spirit into a desert. There I saw a woman sitting on a scarlet beast that was covered with blasphemous names and had seven heads and ten horns.

9 'This calls for a mind with wisdom. <u>The seven heads are seven hills on which the woman sits. 10 They are also seven kings. Five have fallen, one is, the other has not yet come; but when he does come, he must remain for only a little while. 11 The beast who once was, and now is not, is an eighth king</u>. He belongs to the seven and is going to his destruction. 12 '<u>The ten horns you saw are ten kings who</u> have not yet received a kingdom, but who <u>for one hour will receive authority as kings along with the beast. 13 They have one purpose and will give their power and authority to the beast.</u>

In Revelation the whore is described as riding upon a scarlet leopard-like beast. The ancient Babylonian goddess, Ishtar, was regularly depicted as riding on either a leopard or a lion. This similar beast in Revelation is described as having seven heads and ten horns – kind of difficult to picture this!

The meaning of the seven heads is not made immediately clear, although comparing this with the prophecies of Daniel, we can see that they relate to re-incarnations of the same moving empire-spirit down through history – seven different empires all with the same demonic inspiration. Therefore, the seven heads, or seven hills, are in chronological order – they are empires that follow one another down through history:–

- **Egypt,**
- **Assyria**
- **Babylon**
- **Medo-Persia**
- **Greece**
- **Rome**

- **one final beast empire yet to be revealed**

The feature that is more clearly spelled out here is that of the ten horns. Revelation says specifically that these are ten kings, or rulers, who rule alongside the harlot, though initially being under her domination and control. This harlot, – whore, prostitute – is itself a dominant world power. We will identify her in due course, but my previous book – *The Whore and her Mother* – covers this in much more detail.

The whore is called Babylon – specifically *'Mega-Babylon'*, or the *'daughter of Babylon.'* She appears in history before the beast (the 11th horn) and is contemporary with the ten horns of the beast. Eventually, these ten nations will tire of her domination and plot to overthrow Mega-Babylon completely. In plotting her destruction these ten leaders work alongside the beast – he is an integral part of the conspiracy to destroy her, but himself will not be revealed to the world until she is destroyed – *'taken out of the way.'*

> **2 Thessalonians 2:6** And <u>now you know what is holding him back, so that he may be revealed at the proper time</u>. 7 For the secret power of lawlessness is already at work; but <u>the one who now holds it back will continue to do so till he is taken out of the way. 8 And then the lawless one will be revealed</u>, whom the Lord Jesus will overthrow with the breath of his mouth and destroy by the splendour of his coming.

So, the beast is being held back until the *'daughter of Babylon'* – the harlot – *'is taken out of the way.'* The beast, working with these ten rulers of powerful nations, will bring about the complete destruction of Babylon.

> **Revelation 17:15** Then the angel said to me, 'The waters you saw, where the prostitute sits, are peoples, multitudes, nations and languages. 16 <u>The beast and the ten horns you saw will hate the prostitute. They will bring her to ruin and leave her naked; they will eat her flesh and burn her with fire</u>. 17 For God has put it into their hearts to accomplish his purpose by agreeing to hand over to the beast their royal authority, until God's words are fulfilled. 18 The woman you saw is the great city that rules over the kings of the earth.'

Chapter 5 – Woman and a ten-horned beast

Who, then is the *'daughter of Babylon'* – or *'Mega-Babylon'* – this *great city that rules over the kings of the earth.'*? I will give you some criteria to help identify her, which are taken from my book – *The Whore and her Mother.* If you need more convincing than this then I suggest you read that book.

Babylon has to fulfil certain criteria – taken from **Revelation 17,18**, **Jeremiah 50,51** and the other relevant prophecies about Babylon – here is my summary based on these criteria:

Mega-Babylon, the *'daughter of Babylon':*

1. **Ancient Babylon** has no Jewish – or any other – population; is situated hundreds of miles from the sea; and has no involvement – or ever likely to have – with world trade!

2. **Jerusalem** has a significant Jewish population, but is situated on top of mountains, with no access to the sea; and has no significant connection with world trade.

3. **Rome** has very small Jewish population; is not a port, or on the coast; and is not a significant centre for trade or imports.

4. **Brussels** *is* a stock trading centre (though not one of the major ones); it has a very small Jewish population; and has no access to the sea or shipping/imports.

5. **Mecca** is not near the sea, has no Jewish population, is not a mega-city, has no connection with trade, is not a daughter nation and does not dominate the world militarily, or economically – though Saudi Arabia has a strong impact on the world because of its oil.

6. Among those considered, **New York City** is the only mega-city worthy of the name. It also has the world's largest Jewish population (outside of Israel), and is one of the world's major deep water ports, import and immigration centres.

7. The fact that none of the other possible contenders for Mega-Babylon has any kind of sea-port, leaves the major port of **New York City** as the most likely candidate.

8. **New York City** has had not only one, but three, major stock exchanges, dealing in all of the commodities listed in **Revelation** and, specifically, is the major city trading in both gold and diamonds.

9. **New York City** is by far the world's most important port in terms of immigration – or *'bodies and souls of men'*, as **Revelation** puts it.

10. The **United States of America** is the world's strongest economy – importing 43% of the world's resources each year, though with only 6% of the world's population!

11. The **United States of America** is the only world superpower today – dominating every other nation in the world by its military and economic might.

12. The population of the **United States of America** have, by and large, an extremely arrogant and self-centred approach to the rest of the world.

13. **New York City** has, outside of Israel itself (and only then if we include *'greater Tel Aviv'*), the largest Jewish population of any city in the world.

14. The world's only inhabited, *'Town of Babylon'* – founded by immigrant Jews – is situated on Long Island, in the middle of **New York City**.

15. The headquarters of the United Nations is based in Manhattan, another reason why **New York City** is where *'the nations stream!'* (**Jeremiah 51:44**)

16. The **United States of America** regards itself as the *'world's policeman'*, regularly interfering in the affairs of other nations, to the extent even of invading them, and can be accurately described as *'the hammer of the whole earth'*.

17. The United States is the only nation that could be described as both a daughter nation and an empire – the United Kingdom being the *'mother nation.'* (**Jeremiah 50:23**)

My conclusion – based on these criteria – is that New York City is the city described in these prophecies and the United States is the nation.

Chapter 5 – Woman and a ten-horned beast

Back to the ten horns and the beast who will destroy Babylon. We should be looking for nations, therefore, which dominate economically <u>along with</u> Babylon, i.e. alongside the USA.

Many have taken this ten-nation configuration to be a re-constructed Europe – the European Union (EU), Brussels, European Monetary Union, the Euro and all that goes with it. Are they correct? Well, we need also to refer here to the prophecy of the statue in Daniel 2 that we looked at earlier.

The rock – the Kingdom of God – will destroy the spirit of empire once and for all. This statue prophecy is very similar to the seven-headed, ten-horned beast. It depicts four empires stretching forward through history from Daniel's time onward.

Daniel received this revelation while the world was under the Babylonian Empire, (the head of gold), but shortly after that it was toppled by the Medo-Persian Empire, (the shoulders and arms of silver). In turn these were followed by the Greek Empire of Alexander the Great and his followers, (the belly and thighs of bronze), and then the Roman Empire, (the legs of iron).

There is one more empire mentioned by Daniel, the feet of iron mixed with clay – an end-time empire with ten toes containing some of the iron (i.e. from the Roman Empire), but also of clay, (i.e. NOT from the Roman Empire).

Let's consider the *European Union* (formerly the *European Economic Community*), centred on Brussels. The original community was formed by the *Treaty of Rome* – certainly a link there with the *'legs of iron'*.

The community grew to nine nations – it would have been ten, but Norway dropped out, some think partly because of this end-time prophecy of Daniel! The community then became 12, then 25 and is currently composed of 28 nations – with another three under consideration.[*] The UK, of course, is now in the process of leaving the EU.

---

[*] *Wikipedia.org*

Facing the Beast – *Raymond McCullough*

Many of these nations have no conceivable link with the old Roman Empire. Certainly nations such as Italy, France, Spain, Greece and Britain were once under control of Rome, but Sweden, Poland, Ireland, Denmark, Czech Republic, have no such connection. Perhaps the EC does not quite fit – quite apart from it NOT having ten nations!

But think again, if the feet – and ten toes – were composed <u>entirely</u> of iron in Daniel's prophecy, then we would expect to find this union entirely within Europe. But that is clearly NOT the case, the feet are *'of iron <u>mixed</u> with baked clay'* – two things which do not mix, naturally.

Some of these ten nations may have a former link with Rome – the toes of iron; but they are joined by other nations who are *'toes of clay'* and therefore have NO connection with Rome. Where does that leave us, then? Can we relate this to any powerful union which mixes some nations of Europe and other nations outside of Europe, in this way?

One group does spring to mind – not a political union, which many have sought in vain to identify, but a powerful economic union. Heard of the G8? Or indeed the G20? What are these groups? The G8 is considered to be a gathering of the strongest nations of the world, in economic terms.

Who are the members of the G8? Well, we currently have the USA itself, plus Canada, Japan, Russia, <u>United Kingdom, France, Germany, Italy</u>. Wait a minute! Aren't those last four nations former components of the old Roman Empire – United Kingdom, Italy, France and Germany? So we already have four *'toes of iron'* – but we don't have ten nations? Or do we?

Well, if you think about it carefully, we really ought to be looking for a group of eleven nations! Remember that the harlot, who rides upon the beast, is a <u>separate entity</u> from the ten nations who are the horns of the beast? So, we need to think of ten nations – in addition to the USA – i.e. eleven in total.

Let's look more closely at the G8, which holds regular economic summits, each time promising great changes in Africa and other poverty-stricken parts of the world, but never

Chapter 5 – Woman and a ten-horned beast

delivering. Let me stick my neck out and make a prediction! The G8 will <u>never</u> make a significant reduction in poverty, AIDS, malaria, 3rd world debt relief, or any of the things that really matter to the poorest of this world.

They are an organisation of the *'haves'*, with no interest in benefiting the *'have-nots'* of this world! These are the nations most in control of the world's economy, with great power to manipulate things to benefit – not the whole world – but simply themselves!

At the G8 summit in Edinburgh, Scotland, held in 2005 (which friends of mine attended as protesters), there were NOT just eight nations taking part. As well as those eight mentioned above, the premier of <u>China</u> was there, with a high-level representative of the government of <u>India</u>, plus Kofi Annan, then head of the <u>United Nations</u> organisation. That actually <u>does</u> make eleven rulers, doesn't it?

Now, the make-up of the *'G8'* may well change, but it seems a more likely candidate for the *'ten-horned beast'* than the EC itself.

Now we have almost the full club – UK, Germany, France & Italy, (toes of iron); together with Canada, Japan, Russia, China, India and ...? (toes of clay). The fact that we don't have an exact ten nations yet is not terribly important, as some nations may well be added. We already have a wider G20 group, so there are plenty of possibilities to choose from.

And it is still possible that one, or more, of the existing member nations could leave – though that would have to be by divine intervention, I think! I believe the membership of this group will become much clearer, (and stronger), as time goes on. Keep an eye on the development of the *'G8'!*

The characteristics of this ten-horned entity – conglomerate – are that they currently share the goals and influences of Mega-Babylon. They *'share in her luxuries'*, profit greatly from their trade with her, have *'drunken the wine of her fornication'* – meaning they have drifted further and further from any respect for the God of Israel and his *Torah*.

The world globalisation movement involves many more states than simply the USA – in that sense Mega-Babylon is a world-wide phenomenon.

We, in the countries of the West, and many others in Asia, South America and elsewhere, are caught up in this market-economy, globalisation movement – where the very rich get richer, the majority of us get poorer and the poorest suffer greatly! We have all drunk of the wine of her impurity, shared in her luxuries.

We are led by luxuries. Just think for a minute: How many mobile phones has your family purchased in the last 10 years? How many cars? How many luxury electronic items have we purchased? Our grandparents had no need of any of these things and probably lived happier lives, on average.

But the problem with globalisation and the market economy is that more and more of the world's population are being left behind – *'Falling Off the Edge'*, as Alex Perry calls it in his book of the same title.

The God of Israel continually makes it clear in the *Tanakh* that He is concerned with how we treat the poor and under-privileged. He continually upbraids Israel and Judah through his prophets, because of their exploitation of the weak and marginalised.

It is for this very reason that he removed the northern kingdom of Israel – and later also Judah – from the land he had promised to them. (**Amos 2:6,7**; **3:10,11**; **5:11,12**; etc.) He is totally opposed to globalisation, greed and exploitation of the weak, no matter what nation it occurs in! The idea that the God of Israel would be aligned with those in power today is a total distortion of the truth!

Now the members of the G8 group are not yet set in stone. There is still time for a nation – perhaps Canada, the United Kingdom, or whoever – to come to their senses and *'return to their God'*. If Norway could make such a choice about membership of the EU, then it is certainly possible for other nations to change their destiny!

Chapter 5 – Woman and a ten-horned beast

Who are the ten horns?

1. They willingly share with the harlot in her luxuries and fornications, though she is riding on their backs.

2. They are composed partly of iron (linked to the old Roman Empire), but also partly of clay (nations with NO connection with the Roman Empire). Incidentally, this would rule out any direct connection with the European Union (EU).

3. The body which currently best fits the description of these economically strong nations is the G8 economic grouping, which makes decisions for the rest of the world! The numbers don't fit – yet! – but the G8 already involves representatives of China, India and the UN – almost the ten plus one required!

4. There is still just about time for a nation, or nations, to heed God's word and opt out of this evil destiny!

5. The beast, along with the ten horns, will be the means of destruction Mega-Babylon.

6. When the great military and economic super-power of Babylon USA – is *'taken out of the way,'* then there will be nothing left to hinder the beast from being revealed to the world.

Facing the Beast – *Raymond McCullough*

6 – The destroyer of Babylon

Imagine this news broadcast repeating around the world:

'We interrupt this programme to bring you an urgent news bulletin:

'America has been attacked!

'In the early hours of this morning, thousands of missiles and war planes attacked the United States of America. Warplanes are still flying across Canada, but there has been absolutely no response, or counter-attack, from the USA.

All communications from the USA have been cut off since 5 am Eastern Time. We are relying on reports from ships off the coast of the USA, who are reporting fires and smoke all the way along the Atlantic coast as far as the eye can see. Reports are also coming in of further devastation on the Pacific coast.

'I honestly can't believe what I'm reading. This seems like a fairytale, but I repeat, **America has suffered a devastating missile attack!**

'At this stage, we don't know what damage has been inflicted, but military experts say this has the hallmarks of an all out nuclear strike.

'The last news report received by Reuters was of the President attending a major celebration in New York City, expected to continue into the early hours. No communication has been received from there since, but, from the one satellite we still have access to, it would appear that most American cities are now a smoking ruin!

'US satellites are not responding. We have no internet, phone or radio communication whatsoever with the United States. Whatever has happened there is terrifying to contemplate.

Facing the Beast – *Raymond McCullough*

'The world's only superpower appears to have been destroyed – annihilated – in a totally unprecedented attack! We don't know yet if anyone has survived, but there has been absolutely no sign of a counter-attack, or any kind of response, from the US.

'The UK Prime Minister reports that he is dumbfounded with shock. 'I've been trying the hotline to the president all morning', he said, 'there is no reply!'

'Meanwhile, stock markets in London, Brussels, and around the world, have suspended trading indefinitely!'

Now, for a minute, just try to re-run that bulletin and replace the USA with, say, the old favourite, the Roman Catholic Church? How realistic does it sound, now? It makes no sense, does it? Nor does it fit in with the words of the prophets.

How will this fall of America take place? Who will the destroying forces be? Time is running out for the United States and payback time is fast approaching!

Remember, in Revelation, the prophet John describes the prostitute Mega-Babylon as riding upon a scarlet beast, with ten horns and ten crowns on these horns. He describes other attributes of this beast as well, but let's just consider the ten horns for now.

We don't have any difficulty in interpreting their meaning, because the angel in the same chapter clearly interprets it for us!

> **Revelation 17:12** <u>The ten horns you saw are ten kings, who have not yet begun to rule; but they receive power as kings for one hour along with the beast</u>. 13 They have one mind, and they hand over their power and authority to the beast. 16 <u>As for the ten horns that you saw and the beast, they will hate the whore, bring her to ruin, leave her naked, eat her flesh, and consume her with fire.</u> 17 For God put in their hearts to do what will fulfil his purpose, that is, to be of one mind and give their kingdom to the beast, until God's words have accomplished their intent.

Chapter 6 – The destroyer of Babylon

Who do the Hebrew prophets say will carry out this retribution? Firstly, that same ten nation *'beast'* empire which, until now has been carrying Babylon upon its back. Remember, some of the toes, the ones made of iron, are European countries formerly within the ancient Roman Empire.

>**Habakkuk 2:4** "See, he is puffed up; his desires are not upright—but the righteous will live by his faith 5 indeed, wine betrays him; he is arrogant and never at rest. Because he is as greedy as the grave and like death is never satisfied, he gathers to himself all the nations and takes captive all the peoples. 6 "Will not all of them taunt him with ridicule and scorn, saying, "'Woe to him who piles up stolen goods and makes himself wealthy by extortion! <u>How long must this go on?' 7 Will your debtors not suddenly arise? Will they not wake up and make you tremble? Then you will become their victim. 8 Because you have plundered many nations, the peoples who are left will plunder you.</u> For you have shed man's blood; you have destroyed lands and cities and everyone in them.

The fall of Babylon is partly the calling in of her debts. Her creditors will *'suddenly arise.'* The United States of America is continuing to run up a huge balance of payments deficit, currently around 22 trillion dollars! Among the ten powerful nations of the G8 are several who hold those American debts.

Currently, the debt is owed firstly to China, the world's strongest economy at the moment; and secondly, to Japan. Sooner or later the debt will be called in and China, Japan and Russia (which holds a considerable portion of the debt) – along with the other seven nations of the *G10?* – will conspire to militarily overthrow and totally destroy the USA!

This G8/G10 group at present includes Russia, Japan and Germany. Do these nations not include many who still have reasons to be resentful of the USA, and who may have scores to settle for previous military or economic humiliation?

When Russia finally opted for a market economy, during the Clinton era, the USA sent in a high-powered advisor, Richard Armitage, to help the Russians *'transition their economy.'* When he left, $500 billion had somehow disappeared out of the Russian economy, and the Russian government could no longer afford to pay its civil servants, or even the soldiers of the Red Army! Instead, a small number of oligarchs suddenly had tremendous economic power and influence across the country.*

Remember, too, that Russia still has many thousands of nuclear missiles, formerly targeted towards the US. A nuclear strike against US nuclear silos would result in a catastrophe; just look at the current nuclear problems in Japan after the 2010 tsunami.

That resentment against the USA has been building up also in many other parts of the world, especially in the Arab and Moslem states. We've seen that already through the 9/11 attack.

Most of those involved had Saudi Arabian connections, yet no-one in the US administration decided to go to war with Saudi Arabia! In fact, the first people allowed to fly out of the US after 9/11 were members of the Bin Laden family – some of them wanted for questioning by the FBI!

Let's face it, the motivation is already there. The means are available: nuclear weapons in Russia, China and elsewhere. The tools are available: potential terrorists all over the Moslem world, with a readiness to attack the USA from within. All that is required now is the opportunity!

If these forces were to unite and plot together against the USA, what could stop them? Only divine intervention! But if that should no longer be available, then disaster would be inevitable.

> **Jeremiah 51:8** Babylon <u>will suddenly fall</u> and be broken. Wail over her! <u>Get balm for her pain; perhaps she can be healed. 9 "'We would have healed Babylon, but she cannot be healed;</u> let us leave her and each go to our own land, for her judgement reaches to the skies, it rises as high as the heavens.'

This verse seems to describe God's willingness to heal, rather than to judge, Babylon, but the choice is in her own hands.

---

* See chapter 6 of **Crossing the Rubicon**, *Michael Ruppert*

Chapter 6 – The destroyer of Babylon

The prophets clearly describe YHWH's unwillingness to judge nations, even when it is clearly foretold:

> **Jeremiah 18:7** If at any time I announce that a nation or kingdom is to be uprooted, torn down and destroyed, 8 and <u>if that nation I warned repents of its evil, then I will relent and not inflict on it the disaster I had planned.</u> 9 And if at another time I announce that a nation or kingdom is to be built up and planted, 10 and if it does evil in my sight and does not obey me, then I will reconsider the good I had intended to do for it.

> **2 Chronicles 7:14** if my people, who are called by my name, will humble themselves and pray and seek my face and turn from their wicked ways, then I will hear from heaven, and I will forgive their sin and will heal their land.

Of all nations, surely these words apply to the United States right now? Against this we have the clear words of Jeremiah, *"We <u>would have healed Babylon</u>, but she cannot be healed,"* which seems to suggest that maybe things have been left too late for healing?

The USA is today a very divided nation – every effort is being made to bring down the present president and his government. If that should happen, the US will revert very quickly to the policies of the Obama period – and probably go well beyond them. It is then, I believe, that we will see the fulfilment of all the prophecies about Babylon about which we currently think, *'No, the US would never do that.'*

This disaster will take place *"In one hour!"* The prophetic words seem to emphasise the suddenness of her fall – *"Babylon will suddenly fall and be broken."* (**Jeremiah 51:8**)

> **Revelation 18:21** Then a mighty angel picked up a boulder the size of a large millstone and threw it into the sea, and said: "<u>With such violence the great city of Babylon will be thrown down</u>, never to be found again.

> **Jeremiah 50:44** Like a lion coming up from Jordan's thickets to a rich pastureland, <u>I will chase Babylon from its land in an instant</u>.

There will be no time for anyone, military or civilian, to prepare – except, of course, for those who have heeded these prophetic warnings beforehand. There will be protection for those who are remaining alert and prayerful – though what form that protection will take is difficult to predict.

We know approximately who will carry out this attack – at least those who will lead and mastermind it. This will not be a small terrorist group, no matter how well organised. The prophets speak of several nations coming against Babylon – specifically those whom she has been riding upon, the ten nation alliance of economically strong nations.

> **Revelation 17:16** The beast and the ten horns you saw will hate the prostitute. They will bring her to ruin and leave her naked; they will eat her flesh and burn her with fire.

The attack will be led by the *'beast'*, the new world ruler in hiding, accompanied by the ten rulers who will hand over to him and give him his initial authority. This is the conspiracy to end all conspiracies. One man, with the authority of ten of the world's most powerful nations behind him, will plot to attack and totally destroy Mega-Babylon. But there will be plenty of helpers ready to carry out these attacks.

> **Revelation 18:6** Give back to her as she has given; pay her back double for what she has done. Pour her a double portion from her own cup. 7 Give her as much torment and grief as the glory and luxury she gave herself.

There is another international organisation that perhaps we should mention here. It is now known as the *Shanghai Co-operation Organisation* and has boasted that they represent *'half of humanity.'* The six member states at present are China, Russia, Kazakhstan, Kyrgyzstan, Tajikistan and Uzbekistan – with India, Iran, Mongolia and Pakistan having observer status.

There are no European nations involved – so this cannot encompass the ten nation power bloc of Daniel and Revelation, but the gathering together of these nations is certainly ominous.

Where will the main attack be launched from?

Chapter 6 – The destroyer of Babylon

Jeremiah 50:2 <u>Babylon will be captured</u>; Bel will be put to shame, Marduk filled with terror. Her images will be put to shame and her idols filled <u>with terror.</u> 3 <u>A nation from the north will attack her and lay waste her land.</u> No one will live in it; both people and animals will flee away.

9 I will stir up and <u>bring against Babylon an alliance of great nations from the land of the north</u>. They will take up their positions against her, and <u>from the north she will be captured</u>.

41 "<u>Look! An army is coming from the north; a great nation and many kings are being stirred up from the ends of the earth</u>.

Jeremiah 51:48 Then heaven and earth and all that is in them will shout for joy over Babylon, <u>for out of the north destroyers will attack her,</u>" declares the LORD.

An army attacking in battle formation? An alliance of great nations from the land of the north? It looks like the attack will come from the north, perhaps taking thinly populated Alaska first, in order to attack from there. How might this affect Canada?

Jeremiah 51:27 "Lift up a banner in the land! Blow the trumpet among the nations! Prepare the nations for battle against her; summon against her these kingdoms: Ararat, Minni and Ashkenaz. Appoint a commander against her; send up horses like a swarm of locusts. 28 Prepare the nations for battle against her— the kings of the Medes, their governors and all their officials, and all the countries they rule.

Ararat, as we know, is in <u>Turkey</u>. Ashkenaz is thought to refer to <u>Germany</u>, from the fact that Ashenazi, or European, Jews originate from this area. According to the *Jewish Virtual Library*, in medieval rabbinical literature the name Ashkenaz was used for Germany.

The Medes is a reference to Persia, i.e. modern day <u>Iran.</u> No surprises there, then! Some of these nations may already have suffered defeat at the hands of Israel, and so may in turn be ready to take revenge against the US.

Will this include a nuclear attack? It seems likely, according to the description in **Revelation**:

Revelation 18:8 Therefore in one day her plagues will overtake her: <u>death, mourning and famine. She will be consumed by fire</u>, for mighty is the Lord God who judges her. 9 "When the kings of the earth who committed adultery with her and shared her luxury see <u>the smoke of her burning</u>, they will weep and mourn over her. 10 Terrified at her torment, they will stand far off and cry:

Jeremiah 50:32 I will kindle <u>a fire in her towns that will consume all</u> who are around her."

From offshore, witnesses will be able to see Babylon burning. The *'smoke of her burning'* will be visible far out to sea. There will be many witnesses of her destruction.

Jeremiah 50:43 "<u>The king of Babylo</u>n has heard the report about them, And <u>his hands hang limp; Distress has gripped him, Agony like a woman in childbirth</u>.

The attack will come so suddenly that the President will simply be paralysed by the news reports coming in. His great military will be wiped out in one hour! (**Jeremiah 50: 27, 30**)

Jeremiah 50:3 <u>Do not spare her young men</u>; completely destroy her army. **4** <u>They will fall down slain in Babylon, fatally wounded in her streets</u>.

Jeremiah 51:30 <u>Babylon's warriors have stopped fighting; they remain in their strongholds. Their strength is exhausted; they have become weaklings</u>. Her dwellings are set on fire; the bars of her gates are broken. 31 <u>One courier follows another and messenger follows messenger to announce to the king of Babylon that his entire city is captured, 32 the river crossings seized, the marshes set on fire, and the soldiers terrified</u>."

Jeremiah 51:53 "<u>Even if Babylon ascends to the heavens and fortifies her lofty stronghold</u>, I will send destroyers against her," declares YHWH.

Even the USA's weapons in space will not be enough to save her. The United States is the only nation to have a *Star Wars* program of weapons in space.*

In addition to this they have the *HAARP* system (High Frequency Active Auroral Research Program), which can be

---

* **The Guardian** - *www.guardian.co.uk*

Chapter 6 – The destroyer of Babylon

used to influence climate, communications and possibly as a more direct weapon. Russia has already protested about this project.*

For the rest of the world this will be the biggest and most sensational news item ever! The story will flash around the earth, leaving everyone stunned and wondering, *"What happens now?"*

Revelation 18: 46 At the sound of Babylon's capture <u>the earth will tremble; its cry will resound among the nations</u>.

Jeremiah 51:54 "The sound of a cry comes from Babylon, the sound of great destruction from the land of the Babylonians. 55 YHWH will destroy Babylon; he will silence her noisy din. Waves of enemies will rage like great waters; the roar of their voices will resound. 56 A destroyer will come against Babylon; her warriors will be captured, and their bows will be broken. For YHWH is a God of retribution; he will repay in full. 57 <u>I will make her officials and wise men drunk, her governors, officers and warriors as well; they will sleep forever and not awake</u>," declares the King, whose name is YHWH Almighty.

It seems likely that the President and other leaders, including those of the military, will actually be drunk and unable to react when the attack occurs!

Revelation 18:21 Then a mighty angel picked up a boulder the size of a large millstone and threw it into the sea, and said: "<u>With such violence the great city of Babylon will be thrown down, never to be found again</u>.

22 The music of harpists and musicians, pipers and trumpeters, will never be heard in you again.

No worker of any trade will ever be found in you again.

The sound of a millstone will never be heard in you again.

23 The light of a lamp will never shine in you again.

The voice of bridegroom and bride will never be heard in you again.

---

* **Angels Don't Play This HAARP** *Jeane Manning, Dr. Nick Bergich* (Bibliography)

<u>Your merchants were the world's important people.</u> By your magic spell all the nations were led astray. 24 In her was found the blood of prophets and of God's holy people, of all who have been slaughtered on the earth."

How will Babylon fall?

1 She will become the victim of her creditors. Their loan will be called in and they will take revenge on her.

2 The man-beast and the ten rulers who will hand over their authority to him, upon whose back the prostitute has been riding, will hate her, turn on her, *"leave her naked, eat her flesh and burn her with fire."*

3 Her destruction will come suddenly – *"in one hour"*, *"in an instant";* and with great violence. It will take Babylon, her leaders, and the whole world, by surprise.

4 The main attack will come from the north – *"a nation from the north will attack her"*, *"an alliance of great nations from the land of the north"*.

5 The nations involved would seem to include Turkey, Iran (and her satellites) and Germany, along with Russia and China; though these will not be the only nations taking part.

6 The ruler of Babylon will be totally paralysed by the incoming news of the attack and the destruction of his military forces. He will be unable to react and the military will simply give up fighting.

7 Babylon will be *"consumed by fire"*, *"a fire in her towns ... will consume all who are around her"*. The *"smoke of her burning"* will be witnessed from far out to sea. This would seem to indicate nuclear destruction!

8 The news of her destruction will shake the whole world!

7 – The beast is revealed

Jeremiah 50:46 At the shout, "Babylon has been seized!" the earth is shaken, and an outcry is heard among the nations.

As we said in the previous chapter, the news of the fall of Babylon will shock the whole world, leaving the vast majority of people stunned and wondering, *"What on earth happens now?"*

That worldwide sense of shock will continue. The whole earth will have been taken by complete surprise by the fall of Mega-Babylon. No-one expected this. Nobody will know what is happening. Rulers and kings will be at a loss to explain it. Business leaders and merchants will be devastated by the news. Stock markets around the world will fall through the floor!

In what remains of the United States there will be total chaos. But there will be survivors, because we are told what these survivors will do after the fall.

Perhaps outside of the cities there will be less desolation – although the prophecies describe her rivers being dried up, even the animals leaving! Some human life will remain, though – but there may not be much to sustain it for very long.

Jeremiah 50:3 No one will live in it; both people and animals will flee away.

Revelation 18:22 The music of harpists and musicians, pipers and trumpeters, will never be heard in you again.
No worker of any trade will ever be found in you again.
The sound of a millstone will never be heard in you again.
23 The light of a lamp will never shine in you again.
The voice of bridegroom and bride will never be heard in you again.

Jeremiah 50:40 declares YHWH, 'so no one will live there; no people will dwell in it.

Jeremiah 50:29 The land trembles and writhes, for YHWH's purposes against Babylon stand – to lay waste the land of Babylon so that no one will live there.

This does not promise much of a future for those who managed to survive!

Jeremiah 50:38 A drought on her waters! They will dry up.

Jeremiah 51:41 How desolate Babylon will be among the nations! 42 The sea will rise over Babylon; its roaring waves will cover her. 43 Her towns will be desolate, a dry and desert land, a land where no one lives, through which no one travels.

Jeremiah 51:25 "I will stretch out my hand against you, roll you off the cliffs, and make you a burned-out mountain. 26 <u>No rock will be taken from you for a cornerstone, nor any stone for a foundation</u>, for you will be desolate forever," declares YHWH.

There will be no water supply, so no possibility even of subsistence farming, or of eking it out in the woods, or whatever. This place will have become a desert!

Isaiah 13:14 Like a hunted gazelle, like sheep without a shepherd, <u>they will all return to their own people, they will flee to their native land</u>.

Jeremiah 50:16 Because of the sword of the oppressor <u>let everyone return to their own people, let everyone flee to their own land</u>.

Jeremiah 51:9 "'We would have healed Babylon, but she cannot be healed; <u>let us leave her and each go to our own land</u>, for her judgment reaches to the skies, it rises as high as the heavens.'

Survivors will look around at what is left of their country, still being patrolled by their enemies, They will unanimously decide to give up on Babylon and return to their own people and their own lands. They will flee what is left of America.

This could only happen in a land where you have Irish Americans, German Americans, Swedish Americans, Hispanic Americans, African Americans, Chinese Americans, etc. At least there will be a possibility of countries for most people to go back to.

Though what will be the situation of the indigenous First Nations people, who for generations have warned and watched helplessly while their land was being destroyed?

Chapter 7 – The beast is revealed

Of all people, they will have nowhere else to call home. Or will they?

There is already an affinity between Israel and many First Nations people. This link may have grown stronger by the time these events take place, so they may well come to think of Israel as their natural home.

> **Isaiah 14:1** YHWH will have compassion on Jacob; once again he will choose Israel and will settle them in their own land. <u>Foreigners will join them and unite with the descendants of Jacob. 2 Nations will take them and bring them to their own place</u>.

And of course, of the six million Jews who currently live in the United States, there will still be many who have not heeded the warnings of their own scriptures; and yet some will find themselves miraculously still alive afterwards. They are currently being led astray by their own leaders. The prophets speak clearly about their situation:

> **Jeremiah 50:4** "In those days, at that time," declares YHWH, "<u>the people of Israel and the people of Judah together will go in tears to seek YHWH their God. 5 They will ask the way to Zion and turn their faces toward it</u>. They will come and bind themselves to YHWH in an everlasting covenant that will not be forgotten. 6 "<u>My people have been lost sheep; their shepherds have led them astray</u> and caused them to roam on the mountains. They wandered over mountain and hill <u>and forgot their own resting place</u>. 7 Whoever found them devoured them; their enemies said, 'We are not guilty, for they sinned against YHWH, their verdant pasture, YHWH, the hope of their ancestors.' 8 "<u>Flee out of Babylon</u>; leave the land of the Babylonians, and be like the goats that lead the flock.
>
> 18 "I will punish the king of Babylon and his land as I punished the king of Assyria. 19 <u>But I will bring Israel back to their own pasture</u>, and they will graze on Carmel and Bashan; their appetite will be satisfied on the hills of Ephraim and Gilead.
>
> **Jeremiah 51:50** <u>You who have escaped the sword, leave and do not linger!</u> Remember YHWH in a distant land, and call to mind Jerusalem."

Just like they did in Europe after the Nazi holocaust, surviving Jews and Israelites will remember Jerusalem, *'their own resting place'*, *'their own pasture'*, return to YHWH and seek then to get home to Israel – by whatever means there is available!

Jeremiah 50:28 Listen to the fugitives and refugees from Babylon declaring in Zion how YHWH our God has taken vengeance, vengeance for his temple.

The man for the time?

Initially, the world will be in complete chaos, with an economic and political vacuum. World trade will be almost at a standstill, because the one nation which imported 43% of the world's trade goods every year is no longer open for business and will never rise again! Revelation seems to suggest worldwide economic collapse. There will be all kinds of shortages, leading to great hardship and, eventually, famine.

But we will already have a world ruler in waiting. Referred to as *'the beast'* (among many other titles), this man will already have been given the power and authority of ten powerful nations, to attack and destroy the world's only remaining superpower. Now he is poised to *'stand in the gap'*, to fill the political vacuum left after the fall of the United States.

The Messiah can NOT come *'at any moment'*

This man is talked of in both the Hebrew Tanakh and in several places in the New Testament. The apostle, Paul (Shaul) makes a very clear statement to those expecting the Messiah *'at any moment'*:

> **2 Thessalonians 2:1** Concerning the coming of our Lord Jesus Christ and our being gathered to him, we ask you, brothers and sisters, 2 not to become easily unsettled or alarmed by the teaching allegedly from us—whether by a prophecy or by word of mouth or by letter—asserting that the day of the Lord has already come. 3 Don't let anyone deceive you in any way, for that day will not come until the rebellion

occurs and the man of lawlessness is revealed, the man doomed to destruction. 4 He will oppose and will exalt himself over everything that is called God or is worshipped, so that he sets himself up in God's temple, proclaiming himself to be God. 5 Don't you remember that when I was with you I used to tell you these things? 6 And now you know what is holding him back, so that he may be revealed at the proper time. 7 For the secret power of lawlessness is already at work; but the one who now holds it back will continue to do so till he is taken out of the way. 8 And then the lawless one will be revealed, whom the Lord Jesus will overthrow with the breath of his mouth and destroy by the splendour of his coming. 9 The coming of the lawless one will be in accordance with how Satan works. He will use all sorts of displays of power through signs and wonders that serve the lie, 10 and all the ways that wickedness deceives those who are perishing. They perish because they refused to love the truth and so be saved. 11 For this reason God sends them a powerful delusion so that they will believe the lie 12 and so that all will be condemned who have not believed the truth but have delighted in wickedness.

What *'hinders'* the Man being revealed?

Do we know what is holding back Revelation of this man? Who is *"the one who now holds it back"* who *"will continue to do so till he is taken out of the way"* This, says Paul, is when the *'lawless one'* will be revealed. (When Paul calls him the *'Lawless One'*, he means one who is without the *Torah*, or who opposes the *Torah*, the instruction of God.)

Well, who, or what, has just been taken out of the way? The nation of Mega-Babylon, which has dominated the whole world, politically and economically – until now! That world has changed forever and it is now time for this man to be revealed.

Up to this time his plans and alliances (with the ten powerful national rulers) have been necessarily in secret. Now he can safely be revealed, and be proclaimed as the *'saviour of the world'*, the *'hope of the future'*.

In fact, says Paul, '*he will oppose and will exalt himself over everything that is called God or is worshipped, so that he sets himself up in God's temple, proclaiming himself to be God!*'' (**2 Thessalonians 2:**) Paul is referring back to the prophet Daniel's description of the *'king who will exalt himself'* (**Daniel 12:36**). But he won't do that straight away, he will need some time to consolidate his authority across the world, so his approach will be very subtle.

Revelation 14: an end-times summary?

Revelation 14 contains a section where three angels appear in quick succession, each with a different announcement to make. They are referred to as an angel, a second angel and then a third. These, I believe, show us the near future in a nutshell – in chronological order:

> **Revelation 14:6** Then I saw another angel flying in midair, and he had the eternal gospel to proclaim to those who live on the earth—to every nation, tribe, language and people. 7 He said in a loud voice, "Fear God and give him glory, because the hour of his judgement has come. Worship him who made the heavens, the earth, the sea and the springs of water."
>
> 8 A second angel followed and said, "'Fallen! Fallen is Mega-Babylon,' which made all the nations drink the maddening wine of her adulteries."
>
> 9 A third angel followed them and said in a loud voice: "If anyone worships the beast and its image and receives its mark on their forehead or on their hand, 10 they, too, will drink the wine of God's fury, which has been poured full strength into the cup of his wrath. They will be tormented with burning sulphur in the presence of the holy angels and of the Lamb. 11 And the smoke of their torment will rise for ever and ever. There will be no rest day or night for those who worship the beast and its image, or for anyone who receives the mark of its name." 12 This calls for patient endurance on the part of the people of God who keep his commands and remain faithful to Jesus. 13 Then I heard a voice from heaven say, "Write this: Blessed are the dead who die in the Lord from now on." "Yes," says the Spirit, "they will rest from their labour, for their deeds will follow them."

Chapter 7 – The beast is revealed

> 14 I looked, and there before me was a white cloud, and seated on the cloud was one like a son of man with a crown of gold on his head and a sharp sickle in his hand. 15 Then another angel came out of the temple and called in a loud voice to him who was sitting on the cloud, "Take your sickle and reap, because the time to reap has come, for the harvest of the earth is ripe." 16 So he who was seated on the cloud swung his sickle over the earth, and the earth was harvested.

The first angel has the *'eternal good news'* to proclaim to every nation and language. Although many organisations and individuals are zealously working towards this, I don't think any of them would claim that every tribe and tongue has been reached, as yet. So, this is where we are at the moment in this prophetic time-scale.

The second angel announces that *'Babylon is fallen'* – the news of America's destruction that will shock the world; while the third angel gives us a very clear warning against following the *'beast'*, who is about to be revealed. After this, the earth is reaped and the Messiah's kingdom comes into being.

We will also find that Yeshua (Jesus) makes a similar statement in **Matthew 24**, where he talks a lot about his return:

> **Matthew 24:14** <u>This gospel of the kingdom will be preached in the whole world</u> as a testimony to all the nations, <u>and then the end will come.</u>

So, the time-scale is the same. Once the message of the gospel gets out to every nation, things rapidly draw to a close. In fact, there will be only seven years to go! But we'll come to that in a minute.

The *'times of the Gentiles'*

This time that we are currently living in, since the crucifixion, is referred to by the prophets as *'the times of the Gentiles'* (the nations). The *'times of the Gentiles'* began with the crucifixion of Yeshua and will end when every nation, tribe and language has had an opportunity to hear the gospel.

Yeshua prophesied the destruction of Jerusalem, which took place in 70 CE:

> **Luke21:20** "But when you see Jerusalem surrounded by armies, then recognise that her desolation is near. 21 Then those who are in Judea must flee to the mountains, and those who are in the midst of the city must leave, and those who are in the country must not enter the city; 22 because these are days of vengeance, so that all things which are written will be fulfilled. 23 Woe to those who are pregnant and to those who are nursing babies in those days; for there will be <u>great distress upon the land</u> and wrath to this people; 24 and they will fall by the edge of the sword, and will be led captive into all the nations; and Jerusalem will be trampled under foot by the Gentiles <u>until the times of the Gentiles are fulfilled</u>.

After the fall of Jerusalem the Jewish nation were driven from the land and scattered around the world – until recent years. Yeshua used the phrase *'times of the Gentiles'* to refer to a definite period of time, of unspecified length, which will eventually be *'fulfilled'* – in other words, it will come to an end. When it comes to an end, is *'fulfilled'*, the end will come!

Paul (Shaul), in his letter to the Romans, also refers to the *'fulness of the Gentiles'*, meaning when the full number of the Gentiles are added. When this occurs God will turn his attention to Israel.

> **Romans 11:25-26** Blindness in part has happened to Israel until the fullness of the Gentiles be come in. Then ALL ISRAEL shall be saved.

The *'times of the Gentiles'* is a prolonged hiatus in the Messianic time-scale, which is tied up with the destiny of the nation of Israel. The exact time of the Messiah's first coming was revealed to the prophet, Daniel, after he had spent three weeks fasting and praying for the answer.

Daniel's *'Seventy Weeks'*

The prophet Jeremiah before him had foretold that the Jewish captivity in Babylon would last for 70 years. Daniel then sought YHWH about this and was given a very specific answer by the angel, Gabriel, who was sent to enlighten him.

Chapter 7 – The beast is revealed

Daniel 9:20 <u>While I was speaking and praying, confessing my sin and the sin of my people Israel, and making my request to YHWH my God</u> for his holy hill- 21 while I was still in prayer, <u>Gabriel</u>, the man I had seen in the earlier vision, <u>came to me</u> in swift flight about the time of the evening sacrifice. 22 He instructed me and said to me, "Daniel, I have now come to give you insight and understanding. 23 As soon as you began to pray, a word went out, which I have come to tell you, for you are highly esteemed. Therefore, consider the word and understand the vision.

24 "<u>Seventy 'sevens' are decreed for your people and your holy city, to finish transgression, to put an end to sin, to atone for wickedness, to bring in everlasting righteousness, to seal up vision and prophecy and to anoint the Most Holy Place</u>. 25 Know and understand this: <u>from the time the word goes out to restore and rebuild Jerusalem until the Anointed One, the Ruler, comes there will be seven 'sevens,' and sixty-two 'sevens.'</u> It will be rebuilt with streets and a trench, but in times of trouble. 26 <u>After the sixty-two 'sevens,' the Anointed One will be put to death and will have nothing</u>. The people of the ruler who will come will destroy the city and the sanctuary. The end will come like a flood; War will continue to the end, and desolations have been decreed. 27 <u>He will confirm a covenant with many for one 'seven.' In the middle of the 'seven' he will put an end to sacrifice</u> and offering. And at the temple he will set up an abomination that causes desolation, until the end that is decreed is poured out on him."

The seventy *'weeks'* is literally seventy *'sevens'* – in other words, 490 years from Cyrus' decree to Nehemiah to go and rebuild Jerusalem. We only use the word *'weeks'* for convenience because this prophecy is well known as this. Daniel was certainly not expecting to see the Messiah appear after only a year or so!

This period, which relates specifically to the nation of Israel, is divided unequally into two parts by a very important event – after 483 years *'the Messiah will be put to death'* and then immediately follows the *'times of the Gentiles'*. This leaves one *'week'* – seven years – of Daniel's 70 Weeks prophecy then to be fulfilled, once the *'times of the gentiles'* are completed. As Yeshua said:

Matthew 24:14 "This gospel of the kingdom will be preached in the whole world as a testimony to all the nations, and then the end will come."

When the *'times of the Gentiles'* come to an end, then we have only seven more years until Daniel's word is completed and the Messiah comes to set up his kingdom.

As Revelation states, the *'times of the Gentiles'* will end with the fall of Mega-Babylon, and then the man-beast who exalts himself will be revealed and take over the whole world. We return again to the *'times of the Jews'* (or, more accurately, Israelites) for the last *'seven'* (years) of Daniel's prophecy.

Daniel 9:24 "Seventy 'sevens' are decreed for your people and your holy city to finish transgression, to put an end to sin, to atone for wickedness, to bring in everlasting righteousness, to seal up vision and prophecy and to anoint the most holy place.

So, thankfully, the man without law, *'the beast'*, has only seven years to rule! His time will be short, but eventful!

27 He will confirm a covenant with many for one 'seven.' In the middle of the 'seven' he will put an end to sacrifice and offering. And at the temple he will set up an abomination that causes desolation, until the end that is decreed is poured out on him."

After his inauguration before the world by the leaders of the ten powerful nations, almost the first action of the man-beast will be to make a seven-year covenant *'with the many.'* We are not told specifically that this is a covenant with Israel, but the structure of the sentence, and the following statement that he will *'put a stop to sacrifice and grain offering'* does seem to relate specifically to Israel.

The first half of his rule will be spent consolidating his position, *'trampling over the whole earth.'* The whole world will now be in the grip of this arrogant dictator. Then *'in the middle of the week,'* as Daniel says, he will *'put a stop to the temple sacrifices and offerings.'*

Daniel's last *'week'* is divided into two equal halves by the stopping of the temple sacrifice in Jerusalem – something which has not been happening since 70 AD! The three

Chapter 7 – The beast is revealed

and a half year period following this event is referred to many times by the prophets.

Will the Jewish temple be rebuilt?

It would seem that it will be at this point in time that the temple will be rebuilt. There can be no sacrifices or grain offering unless a Jewish temple exists in which to carry out these offerings. Preparations are already well underway for the possibility of this happening. *Cohanim* (priests) are being located around the world and trained in how to offer sacrifices.

The gold and other vessels have been created, ready to carry out the various temple duties. The golden Menorah has been created and is on display in the Jewish Quarter of the Old City in Jerusalem. Cornerstones have been quarried and shaped ready to begin the construction.

The only problem is that the supposed temple site already contains two Moslem mosques – the Dome of the Rock and the Al Aqsa Mosque – and is presently under control of the Moslem *Wakf*. Jews (or Christians) are not even allowed to pray on the Temple Mount at present.

However, there is evidence – for those who wish to look for it (see Bibliography) – that the so-called '*Temple Mount*' was never the site of the Jewish temple, in fact, it was the site of the Roman *Antonia Fortress* and that is why it was preserved for hundreds of years, while the actual temple – and the rest of the city – was totally destroyed, *'not one stone here will be left on another; every one will be thrown down,'* Yeshua prophesied (**Matthew 24:32, Mark 13:2, Luke 19:44, 21:6**).

How will the Antichrist be revealed?

1 There will be some survivors after the fall of Babylon – but nothing will remain to sustain them in that land anymore. They will flee from enemy patrols and return to their own lands.

2 Jews and Israelites who did not heed the warnings of their own prophets will repent, turn to YHWH, and seek to return home to Israel, *'their own resting place.'*

3 The Messiah will not come until the *'man opposed to God's law'* is revealed. Then we have seven years to go!

4 He will not be revealed until *'he who hinders is taken out of the way'*, i.e. until Mega-Babylon is fallen. As he and his ten nation alliance are the main instruments of her destruction, his existence will necessarily be kept secret until after the event.

5 As it is the Antichrist *'beast'* who instigates the destruction of Mega-Babylon, <u>the two cannot be one and the same thing</u>! Babylon rides upon the beast, until the beast turns and completely destroys her.

6 **Revelation 14** gives us a quick summary of the end times; the gospel will reach every nation, tribe and language; Mega-Babylon will fall, and then the Antichrist will be revealed.

6 The *'times of the Gentiles'* are completed with the fall of Babylon and revelation of the Antichrist. Yeshua said, *"Then the end will come".*

7 He exalts himself and is defined by his opposition to anything that is called God, therefore the title, *'antichrist'* – incidentally, a good reason why he may not be a Moslem, either!

8 His covenant *'with many'* will result in the Jewish Temple being rebuilt in Jerusalem, though after 3½ years he will call a halt to the sacrifices.

9 His rule will be the last seven years of Daniel's *'Seventy Weeks'* prophecy, though he only has authority to blaspheme God and to trample the holy city for forty-two months, i.e. three and a half years, 1260 days. As Daniel says, *"He will rule for only a short time."*

8 – The mark of the beast

Revelation 14:9 <u>A third angel</u> followed them and said in a loud voice: "<u>If anyone worships the beast and its image and receives its mark on their forehead or on their hand, 10 they, too, will drink the wine of God's fury</u>, which has been poured full strength into the cup of his wrath. They will be tormented with burning sulphur in the presence of the holy angels and of the Lamb. 11 And the smoke of their torment will rise for ever and ever. There will be no rest day or night for those who worship the beast and its image, or for anyone who receives the mark of its name." 12 This calls for patient endurance on the part of the people of God who keep his commands and remain faithful to Jesus.

The *'beast'*, or antichrist, will cause everyone under his rule to receive a mark. God's wrath will be poured out upon all those who receive this mark, therefore NOT a good idea to receive it? Well, it certainly isn't – but there's more to it than that. Refusing to receive the mark will bring dire consequences from those who govern under the beast. That is why:

12 <u>This calls for patient endurance on the part of the people of God</u> who keep his commands and remain faithful to Jesus.

Revelation 13 gives more details of the beast and this mark:

Revelation 13:1 The dragon stood on the shore of the sea. And I saw a beast coming out of the sea. It had ten horns and seven heads, with ten crowns on its horns, and on each head a blasphemous name. 2 The beast I saw resembled a leopard, but had feet like those of a bear and a mouth like that of a lion. The dragon gave the beast his power and his throne and great authority. 3 <u>One of the heads of</u>

<u>the beast seemed to have had a fatal wound, but the fatal wound had been healed.</u> The whole world was filled with wonder and followed the beast. 4 People worshipped the dragon because he had given authority to the beast, and they also worshipped the beast and asked, "Who is like the beast? Who can wage war against it?" 5 <u>The beast was given a mouth to utter proud words and blasphemies and to exercise its authority for forty-two months</u>. 6 It opened its mouth to blaspheme God, and to slander his name and his dwelling place and those who live in heaven. 7 <u>It was given power to wage war against God's holy people and to conquer them</u>. And it was given authority over every tribe, people, language and nation. 8 <u>All inhabitants of the earth will worship the beast</u>—all whose names have not been written in the Lamb's book of life, the Lamb who was slain from the creation of the world. 9 Whoever has ears, let them hear. 10 "If anyone is to go into captivity, into captivity they will go. If anyone is to be killed with the sword, with the sword they will be killed." This calls for patient endurance and faithfulness on the part of God's people.

11 Then I saw <u>a second beast, coming out of the earth</u>. It had two horns like a lamb, but it spoke like a dragon. 12 It exercised all the authority of the first beast on its behalf, and made the earth and its inhabitants worship the first beast, whose fatal wound had been healed. 13 And it performed great signs, even causing fire to come down from heaven to the earth in full view of the people. 14 <u>Because of the signs it was given power to perform on behalf of the first beast, it deceived the inhabitants of the earth</u>. It ordered them to set up an image in honour of the beast who was wounded by the sword and yet lived. 15 The second beast was given power to give breath to the image of the first beast, so that the image could speak and cause all who refused to worship the image to be killed. 16 <u>It also forced all people, great and small, rich and poor, free and slave, to receive a mark on their right hands or on their foreheads, 17 so that they could not buy or sell unless they had the mark, which is the name of the beast or the number of its name</u>. 18 This calls for wisdom. <u>Let the person who has insight calculate the number of the beast, for it is the number of a man. That number is 666.</u>

The man-beast antichrist has characteristics of the leopard, the bear and the lion; reminiscent of the lion, bear

Chapter 8 – The mark of the beast

and leopard of Daniel 7, which represented the empires of ancient Babylon, Medo-Persia and Greece. He receives great power and authority from the dragon, or Satan.

He is an arrogant narcissist. He wants the whole world to worship him and he will set up the apparatus for this to be carried out. He appears to have been fatally wounded, then healed, causing the world to be *'filled with wonder'* at him.

His right hand man, the false prophet, will do great signs and wonders to deceive and convince the world that they should worship the beast. Those who don't know any better will be forced to fall down before an image of himself, on pain of death, if they refuse!

The false prophet *'had two horns like a lamb, but it spoke like a dragon'* – that might be a clue to the nature of the false prophet. Islam believes that Jesus never died, that he is presently in heaven (true!) and will come back to earth to convert everyone to Islam, claiming that he was really a Moslem all along.

You could see that if a prophet appeared and seemed to do miracles, claiming to be Jesus returned from heaven as promised, that many people might be taken in by this. That is what the prophesies say will happen – great deception. *'Because of the signs it was given power to perform* – even to *'give breath to the image' of the first beast'* – *'it deceived the inhabitants of the earth,'* but it will *'perform on behalf of the first beast,'* – everything he does will work towards causing everyone to worship the first beast.

Not only that, but they are forced to receive a mark to signify that they worship the beast. Without this mark no-one will be able to buy or sell. The scarcest commodity will be food, and without the mark no-one will be able to buy any food.

How can we live, then, if we refuse to accept the mark? The short answer is that many will not! They will be executed for refusing this mark, as an example to others. Even if they are far enough away from the beast's kingdom (the ten nations we've talked about) to escape death, we will need to trust in God's miraculous provision and protection simply to survive.

Many people believe that the *'mark'* refers to the insertion of an RFID chip under the skin to identify and keep tabs on each person, in the same way that we do with our pets at the moment. Those rich people who are afraid of their children being kidnapped have used this technology on their offspring, so that they can be tracked if the worst happens.

As this chip can store data, it could be used to replace the credit card so that no-one could buy or sell without it. This *may* be what it means – but I really don't know the answer to that.

666 – the number of the beast

The mark represents the name of the beast, or the number of his name, which, we are told, is 666! There has been so much crazy speculation over this number and what exactly it means. All kinds of people have been found to fit this number, by substituting numbers (*gematria*) for the letters of a name and then adding this up to get 666.

Suggestions have included the emperor Nero, Mohammed, and the Roman Catholic papacy. Personally, I think such people are adding two and two and getting five!

Here is a thought. Where is the very first place we should look for this number? Would that not be in the Hebrew scriptures themselves? Does this number ever appear anywhere else, apart from Revelation? Yes, it does – three times, in total. The number appears in the books of Kings and Chronicles, both stating the exact same information:

> **1 Kings 10:14 (2 Chronicles 9:13)** The weight of the gold that Solomon received yearly was <u>666 talents</u>.

Well, those verses do contain the number and a name, *Solomon*. In the third instance, strangely enough, it is also contained in a list of names of families who returned from Babylon. In the books of Ezra and Nehemiah we have two very similar lists, but a few people were born in between the

Chapter 8 – The mark of the beast

two numberings, so there is a little variation. So, only in **Ezra 2:13** do we read, '*Of Adonikam 666.*'

What does this mean? Who is Adonikam? I don't know. It's simply a Hebrew name, but if I happen to come across someone called Adonikam – or even, Solomon Adonikam – with apparent political ambitions, I'm certainly gonna give him a wide berth! In my *'Six Hours'* fiction series – based on prophecy – I have used the name Adonikam Suleiman for the beast, but that is simply fiction.

Seriously, all I know is that the scripture says that 666 is '*the number of a man,*' who is the beast, the antichrist – and these are the only places in the scriptures where this number appears directly against a man's name.

Earlier we looked at Daniel's dream of four great beasts, each representing a different empire. (**Daniel 7:2-6**) In a similar way to Revelation, Daniel's dream describes four empires that will rule the known world. He was living in the reign of Belshazzar, king of Babylon, so the first beast represented the empire of Babylon; the second, the Medo-Persian Empire; and the third the Greek Empire, which split into four separate kingdoms after the death of Alexander.

> **Daniel 7:7** "After that, in my vision at night I looked, and there before me was <u>a fourth beast—terrifying and frightening and very powerful. It had large iron teeth; it crushed and devoured its victims and trampled underfoot whatever was left. It was different from all the former beasts, and it had ten horns</u>.

The fourth beast was the coming Roman Empire, conquering in all directions, with teeth of iron, similar to the iron toes in Daniel's statue vision. But, just as Alexander's Greek Empire (the leopard with four wings and four heads) divided into four kingdoms, so this empire develops ten horns – which seems to jump us forward in time to the last days, when the ten strong nations will give their authority to another ruler – the man who opposes God's law (*Torah*).

> **Daniel 7:8** "While I was thinking about the horns, there <u>before me was another horn, a little one, which came up among them; and three of the first horns were uprooted before</u>

<u>it. This horn had eyes like the eyes of a human being and a mouth that spoke boastfully</u>.

Again we have this man, speaking boastfully, and taking over the authority of the ten rulers. We learn here that he will uproot three of the horns. Three of these rulers are overcome by force. Perhaps they are appalled by the direction in which *'the beast'* is taking the world, and object – only to be put down forcefully?

> **Daniel 7:9** "As I looked, "thrones were set in place, and the Ancient of Days took his seat. His clothing was as white as snow; the hair of his head was white like wool. His throne was flaming with fire, and its wheels were all ablaze. **10** A river of fire was flowing, coming out from before him. Thousands upon thousands attended him; ten thousand times ten thousand stood before him. The court was seated, and the books were opened.

The final outcome will be the destruction of the man-beast and the end of his kingdom. Instead, the kingdom of God will take over.

> **Daniel 7:11** "Then I continued to watch because of the boastful words the horn was speaking. I kept looking until the beast was slain and its body destroyed and thrown into the blazing fire. 12 (The other beasts had been stripped of their authority, but were allowed to live for a period of time.) 13 "In my vision at night I looked, and there before me was one like a <u>son of man</u>, coming with the clouds of heaven. He approached the Ancient of Days and was led into his presence. 14 He was given authority, glory and sovereign power; <u>all nations and peoples of every language worshipped him</u>. His dominion is an everlasting dominion that will not pass away, and his kingdom is one that will never be destroyed.

The *'son of man'* is a common description of the Jewish Messiah, and was the title Yeshua used most often to describe himself. Notice that, although he is the *'son of man'*, he is actually worshipped by people of every nation. His kingdom will continue forever!

Daniel asks Gabriel for more explanation about this fourth beast, the ten horns and the little horn.

Chapter 8 – The mark of the beast

Daniel 7:21 As I watched, <u>this horn was waging war against the holy people and defeating them</u>, 22 until the Ancient of Days came and pronounced judgment in favour of the holy people of the Most High, and the time came when they possessed the kingdom.

The little horn, man-beast is most often defined in terms of what he is against, which is why we often refer to him as the antichrist, or anti-Messiah. He wages war against God's people and defeats them. He exalts himself above all that is called God and is opposed to God's law, the *Torah*.

Daniel 7:23 "He gave me this explanation: 'The fourth beast is a fourth kingdom that will appear on earth. It will be different from all the other kingdoms and will devour the whole earth, trampling it down and crushing it. 24 The ten horns are ten kings who will come from this kingdom. After them another king will arise, different from the earlier ones; he will subdue three kings. 25 <u>He will speak against the Most High and oppress his holy people and try to change the set times and the laws. The holy people will be delivered into his hands for a time, times and half a time</u>. 26 "'But the court will sit, and his power will be taken away and completely destroyed forever. 27 Then the sovereignty, power and greatness of all the kingdoms under heaven will be handed over to the holy people of the Most High. His kingdom will be an everlasting kingdom, and <u>all rulers will worship and obey him</u>.'

Not only will the antichrist exalt himself and *"speak against the Most High and oppress His people"*, but he will *"try to change the set times and the laws"*. This is what the Roman emperor, Constantine, did in 385 CE, when he changed the Sabbath (Shabbat) to Sunday, and replaced the biblical, Jewish feasts (Passover, Trumpets and Tabernacles) with the pagan festivals (sun god worship) of Easter and Christmas.*

Unfortunately, over the centuries Christianity – with the exception of the early US pilgrims – has continued to take these pagan celebrations on board and have distanced themselves from the biblical feasts ordained by God in the scriptures. Most Christians are not even aware of the horrible pagan origins of the festivals we celebrate!

---

* <u>en.wikipedia.org</u>,

But, thankfully, his time is limited. He will halt the sacrifices in the *"middle of the 'seven'"*, halfway through the seven year period of his reign. In this passage that time span is referred to as *"a time, times and half a time"* – three and a half years. Over and over in Daniel and in Revelation we find this three and a half year period referred to in several different ways:

"*In the midst of the 'seven'*" he will cut off the sacrifice (**Daniel 9:27**); the holy people will be delivered into his hands for '*time, times and half a time*' (**Daniel 7:25**); the nations will trample the city for '*42 months*' (**Revelation 11:2**); the two witnesses will prophesy for '*1,260 days,*' (**Revelation 11:3**); the woman (Israel) will be hidden in the desert for '*1,260 days*' (**Revelation 12:6**) and also '*for time, times and half a time,*' (**Revelation 12:14**); and the beast will have authority to act for '*42 months.*' (**Revelation 13:5**)

These scriptures all refer in different ways to the same period of time. Halfway through the week (seven) = 3½ years = 42 months = 1,260 days (Jewish calendar, 30 day months). The prophetic scriptures are making something very clear here – that this is a very specific period of time!

In Daniel 8 the angel, Gabriel, expands the description of the man-beast's rule:

> **Daniel 8:23** "In the latter part of their reign [the four horns after Alexander], when rebels have become completely wicked, <u>a fierce-looking king, a master of intrigue, will arise</u>. 24 <u>He will become very strong, but not by his own power</u>. He will cause astounding devastation and will succeed in whatever he does. <u>He will destroy those who are mighty, the holy people</u>. 25 He will cause deceit to prosper, and he will consider himself superior. When they feel secure, he will destroy many <u>and take his stand against the Prince of princes</u>. Yet he will be destroyed, but not by human power. 26 "The vision of the evenings and mornings that has been given you is true, but seal up the vision, for <u>it concerns the distant future</u>."

The '*evenings and mornings*' time period given here – 2,300 days – is NOT about the length of time of the antichrist's rule, it also includes the time taken to cleanse the sanctuary, which will take a certain period of time after the Antichrist is wiped out. (**Daniel 8:13, 14**)

The rock, which represents the kingdom of God, strikes the statue on the feet of iron and clay – and the whole statue is then destroyed and the pieces swept away without leaving a trace! The world empire of the antichrist will be destroyed by the coming of the Messiah's kingdom. And these empires will never rise again!

The Mark of the Beast

1 On behalf of the beast, and as a sign of worshipping the beast, the false prophet will force everyone to receive a mark, on their forehead or right hand, without which they will not be able to buy or sell. The false prophet may claim to be Yeshua come back from heaven.

2 The wrath of God will be poured out upon all those who receive this mark.

3 The mark represents the name of the antichrist, or the number of his name – the number being 666!

4 Playing around with numbers representing letters and words has produced many and varied results – not the most reliable! Suffice to say that this method really produces no definite result.

5 For what it's worth, the Hebrew scriptures only record that number on three occasions – twice with the name, *Solomon*; and once the name, *Adonikam*.

6 The final *'beast'* empire is different from all that went before and tramples the whole world underfoot – in the process throwing down three of the ten powerful nations which have given him his authority. Perhaps they realised too late, where things were heading?

7 Halfway through the seven years of his rule he will take away the sacrifice, set up the *'abomination of desolation'* in the Jewish temple, and *'make war on'* the Jews and believers in Yeshua. This period is also described as 42 months, *'time, times and half a time,'* or 1,260 days – all the same time period.

8 After this, he and his empire will come to an abrupt end when the Messiah returns to set up His kingdom.

9 – The Great Tribulation

This desecration of the temple (**Daniel 11:31**), setting up the *'abomination that causes desolation,'* is what begins the beast's war against the people God – often known as the *'great tribulation,'* the *'time of Jacob's trouble.'*

> **Jeremiah 30:1** This is the word that came to Jeremiah from YHWH: 2 'This is what YHWH, the God of Israel, says: "Write in a book all the words I have spoken to you. 3 The days are coming," declares YHWH, "when I will bring my people Israel and Judah back from captivity and restore them to the land I gave to their ancestors to possess," says YHWH.' 4 These are the words YHWH spoke concerning Israel and Judah: 5 'This is what YHWH says: "'Cries of fear are heard – terror, not peace. 6 Ask and see: can a man bear children? Then why do I see every strong man with his hands on his stomach like a woman in labour, every face turned deathly pale? 7 How awful that day will be! No other will be like it. It will be a time of trouble for Jacob, but he will be saved out of it.

Let's focus for a minute on this period of half a *'seven'* – the three and a half years of the Antichrist's domination of Israel and of God's people. This period of time is mentioned a total of seven times in the books of Daniel and Revelation – plus another mention, in **Daniel 11**, of a period of 1290 days (i.e. with one extra month added).

Let's list these verses to see what can be derived from them, since this period is going to be the ultimate summing up of the age, prior to the triumphant advent of the Messiah, and the beginning of his righteous reign over the whole earth.

> **Daniel 9:26** The people of the ruler who will come will destroy the city and the sanctuary. The end will come like a flood: war will continue until the end, and desolations have been decreed. 27 He will confirm a covenant with many for one 'seven'. In the middle of the 'seven' he will put an end to sacrifice and offering. And on a wing of the temple he will

set up an abomination that causes desolation, until the end that is decreed is poured out on him.

The antichrist will begin his reign with a covenant, an agreement that will allow the Jewish temple to be re-built in Jerusalem and sacrifices and offerings to re-commence.

He will break this covenant and begin his campaign of terror in the middle of the seven years, by putting an end to the temple sacrifices and offerings, and setting up the '*abomination which causes desolation*' – obviously an object which is completely forbidden to the Jews, such as an idol, or image of himself.

> **Daniel 7:24** The ten horns are ten kings who will come from this kingdom. After them another king will arise, different from the earlier ones; he will subdue three kings. 25 He will speak against the Most High and oppress his saints and try to change the set times and the laws. <u>The saints will be handed over to him for a time, times and half a time</u>.

For three and a half years he will speak out against God and oppress the saints, and attempt to change times and laws – as he perhaps realises that these things (i.e. the Jewish feasts) may themselves be prophetic? The saints will be handed over to him for '*time, times and half a time*' – i.e. the same 3½ year period. We will come back to Daniel in a minute. Let's look at what Revelation has to say:

> **Revelation 11:2** But exclude the outer court; do not measure it, <u>because it has been given to the Gentiles. They will tramp on the holy city for 42 months</u>.

The antichrist and his army will '*trample on*' – occupy – Jerusalem for 42 months = three and a half years, once again.

The two witnesses

> **Revelation 11:3** And <u>I will give power to my two witnesses, and they will prophesy for 1,260 days</u>, clothed in sackcloth.

During this period of 1,260 days two prophets will begin to prophecy in Jerusalem. They will have power to stop rain, turn rivers into blood and cause plagues on earth. No-one will be able to harm them for that time, but at the end of this time they will be killed, their bodies displayed for three and a half days, and then they will be resurrected and ascend into heaven.

The woman in the desert

> **Revelation 12:6** The woman fled into the desert to a place prepared for her by God, <u>where she might be taken care of for 1,260 days</u>.
>
> **Revelation 12:14** The woman was given the two wings of a great eagle, so that she might <u>fly to the place prepared for her in the desert, where she would be taken care of for a time, times and half a time</u>, out of the serpent's reach.

Again, we have the same time span – 1,260 days, or *'time, times and half a time'* – when the woman, representing the nation of Israel, will be protected in the wilderness. She will be pursued by the dragon – Satan – who has tried for centuries, without success, to wipe out the nation of Israel.

God has a place prepared for Israel to flee into the desert – perhaps in former Jordan (*'Edom, Moab and ... Ammon will be delivered from his hand'* – **Daniel 11:41**) so Satan will spend his time *'making war'* with the rest of those who follow Yeshua. (**Revelation 12:17**)

The Great Tribulation

> **Revelation 13:5** The beast was given a mouth to utter proud words and blasphemies <u>and to exercise his authority for forty-two months</u>. 6 He opened his mouth to blaspheme God, and to slander his name and his dwelling place and those who live in heaven. 7 <u>He was given power to make war against the saints and to conquer them</u>. And he was given authority over every tribe, people, language and nation. 8 All inhabitants of the earth will worship the beast – all whose names are not written in the book of life belonging to the Lamb that was slain from the creation of the world.

Facing the Beast – *Raymond McCullough*

This persecution of believers in Yeshua will last for that same time period – 42 months – and is usually referred to as the *Great Tribulation*. *'All inhabitants of the earth will worship the beast'* and believers will be persecuted for refusing to worship him.

Jeremiah 30:3 The days are coming,' declares YHWH, 'when I will bring my people Israel and Judah back from captivity and restore them to the land I gave their ancestors to possess,' says YHWH." 4 These are the words YHWH spoke concerning Israel and Judah: 5 "This is what YHWH says: "'Cries of fear are heard— terror, not peace. 6 Ask and see: Can a man bear children? Then why do I see every strong man with his hands on his stomach like a woman in labor, every face turned deathly pale? 7 <u>How awful that day will be! No other will be like it. It will be a time of trouble for Jacob, but he will be saved out of it.</u> 8 "'In that day,' declares YHWH Almighty, 'I will break the yoke off their necks and will tear off their bonds; no longer will foreigners enslave them. 9 Instead, they will serve YHWH their God and David their king, whom I will raise up for them.

This will be the time of Jacob's trouble, but *'he will be saved out of it!'*

Daniel 12:1 "At that time Michael, the great prince who protects your people, will arise. <u>There will be a time of distress such as has not happened from the beginning of nations until then</u>. But at that time your people—everyone whose name is found written in the book—will be delivered.

2 Multitudes who sleep in the dust of the earth will awake: some to everlasting life, others to shame and everlasting contempt. 3 Those who are wise will shine like the brightness of the heavens, and those who lead many to righteousness, like the stars for ever and ever.

At the end of the 3½ years Jacob – *'your people'* – will be delivered. How? *'At that time Michael, the great prince who protects your people, will arise.'* Then the resurrection of the dead to everlasting life will take place. Remember what the apostle Paul told us:

1 Thessalonians 4:15 According to the Lord's word, we tell you that <u>we who are still alive</u>, who are left until the coming of the Lord, <u>will certainly not precede those who</u>

Chapter 9 – The Great Tribulation

have fallen asleep. 16 For the Lord himself will come down from heaven, with a loud command, with the voice of the archangel and with the trumpet call of God, and the dead in Christ will rise first. 17 After that, we who are still alive and are left will be caught up together with them in the clouds to meet the Lord in the air. And so we will be with the Lord for ever. 18 Therefore encourage one another with these words.

So, when the *'multitudes who sleep in the dust of the earth awake ... to everlasting life,'* (**Daniel 12:2**) then *'we who are still alive and are left will be caught up together with them in the clouds to meet the Lord in the air.'* (**1 Thessalonians 4:17**)

> **Revelation 20:4** And I saw the souls of those who had been beheaded because of their testimony about Jesus and because of the word of God. They had not worshipped the beast or its image and had not received its mark on their foreheads or their hands. They came to life and reigned with Christ for a thousand years. 5 (The rest of the dead did not come to life until the thousand years were ended.) This is the first resurrection. 6 Blessed and holy are those who share in the first resurrection. The second death has no power over them, but they will be priests of God and of Christ and will reign with him for a thousand years.

We should point out something here that ought to be quite obvious, but may not be because of wrong teaching – those souls beheaded by the antichrist were killed *'because of their testimony about Jesus,'* they were believers in Yeshua. Brothers and sisters we need to be prepared to endure persecution – just as believers throughout the world today are enduring it. The idea that those who live in the west will not experience persecution is definitely NOT scriptural!

Now, let's go back to Daniel 12:

Daniel 12:5 Then I, Daniel, looked, and there before me stood two others, one on this bank of the river and one on the opposite bank. 6 One of them said to the man clothed in linen, who was above the waters of the river, "How long will it be before these astonishing things are fulfilled?"

7 The man clothed in linen, who was above the waters of the river, lifted his right hand and his left hand toward heaven, and I heard him swear by him who lives forever,

saying, "<u>It will be for a time, times and half a time. When the power of the holy people has been finally broken, all these things will be completed</u>."

8 I heard, but I did not understand. So I asked, "My lord, what will the outcome of all this be?" 9 He replied, "Go your way, Daniel, because <u>the words are rolled up and sealed until the time of the end</u>. 10 Many will be purified, made spotless and refined, but the wicked will continue to be wicked. None of the wicked will understand, but those who are wise will understand.

11 "<u>From the time that the daily sacrifice is abolished and the abomination that causes desolation is set up, there will be 1,290 days. 12 Blessed is the one who waits for and reaches the end of the 1,335 days</u>. 13 "As for you, go your way till the end. You will rest, and then at the end of the days you will rise to receive your allotted inheritance."

Before we miss it let us note an important point that the angel says, *'Many will be purified, made spotless and refined, but the wicked will continue to be wicked. None of the wicked will understand, but those who are wise will understand.'* Through persecution the church will become *'without stain or wrinkle or any other blemish, but holy and blameless,'* as Paul tells us in Ephesians:

Ephesians 5:25 Christ loved the church and gave himself up for her 26 to make her holy, cleansing her by the washing with water through the word, 27 and <u>to present her to himself as a radiant church, without stain or wrinkle or any other blemish, but holy and blameless</u>.

Back to Daniel – again we have this period of *'time, times and half a time,'* denoting the same 3½ year period but, in verse 11, the angel refers to a period of 1,290 days, and a total of 1,335 days. He also tells us that only those who are wise will understand. The two figures represent an extra 30 days, i.e. one Hebrew month, plus another 45 days – 1½ Hebrew months.

There are many explanations of why these extra periods are mentioned – the pouring out of God's wrath upon antichrist's kingdom, to bury the dead, to cleanse the temple, to judge and reward the righteous – but I don't claim to have the answer to that one just yet! Daniel is told by Gabriel that

Chapter 9 – The Great Tribulation

the words are *'sealed until the time of the end,'* so we may not understand until the time is right.

Matthew 24:15 So when you see standing in the holy place 'the abomination that causes desolation', spoken of through the prophet Daniel— let the reader understand— 16 then let those who are in Judea flee to the mountains. 17 Let no-one on the roof of his house go down to take anything out of the house. 18 Let no-one in the field go back to get his cloak. 19 How dreadful it will be in those days for pregnant women and nursing mothers! 20 Pray that your flight will not take place in winter or on the Sabbath. 21 For then there will be great distress, unequalled from the beginning of the world until now— and never to be equalled again. 22 If those days had not been cut short, no-one would survive, but for the sake of the elect those days will be shortened.

Yeshua seems to be referring to Daniel 12:1, which says pretty much the same thing: *'There will be a time of distress such as has not happened from the beginning of nations until then.'* The *'great distress'* is also translated *'great tribulation'* and Yeshua states that it will begin when the *'abomination of desolation,'* spoken of by Daniel, stands in the Holy Place.

Revelation 7:9 After this I looked, and there before me was a great multitude that no one could count, from every nation, tribe, people and language, standing before the throne and before the Lamb. They were wearing white robes and were holding palm branches in their hands. 10 And they cried out in a loud voice:

"Salvation belongs to our God, who sits on the throne, and to the Lamb." 11 All the angels were standing around the throne and around the elders and the four living creatures. They fell down on their faces before the throne and worshipped God, 12 saying: "Amen! Praise and glory and wisdom and thanks and honour and power and strength be to our God for ever and ever. Amen!" 13 Then one of the elders asked me, "These in white robes—who are they, and where did they come from?" 14 I answered, "Sir, you know." And he said, "These are they who have come out of the great tribulation; they have washed their robes and made them white in the blood of the Lamb. 15 Therefore, "they are before the throne of God and serve him day and night in his temple; and he who sits on the throne will shelter them with his presence. 16 'Never again will they hunger; never again will they thirst. The sun will not beat down on them,' nor any scorching heat. 17 For the Lamb at the centre of the throne will be their shepherd; 'he will lead them to springs of living water.' 'And God will wipe away every tear from their eyes.'"

'A great multitude that no one could count, from every nation, tribe, people and language ... [will] come out of the great tribulation.' These are not Jewish believers, they are a huge multitude of Gentiles! Yeshua promised:

> **Matthew 24:22** If those days had not been cut short, no one would survive, but for the sake of the elect those days will be shortened.

A Secret Rapture?

And by the way, John obviously forgot to mention the other *'great multitude'* who were beamed up in the secret rapture – didn't he? Actually, it was because they don't exist! But doesn't the Bible teach that all the righteous are going to be caught up out of all this tribulation? Surely we don't need to be worried about that?

Unfortunately, far too many of those who call themselves *'Christians'* are burying their heads in the sand and hoping that they will never have to endure persecution – never mind death – for their faith. They forget that *'in fact, everyone who wants to live a godly life in Christ Jesus will be persecuted,"!* (**2 Timothy 3:12**) More believers have been martyred this century than in any previous century.* Do we suppose that only we in the West are to be exempt from persecution?

What is the basis for this belief in a secret rapture? Firstly, the word *'rapture'* is an archaic word taken from the phrase meaning to be *'caught up'*, or *'taken up'*. The reference is to those who are still alive when the Messiah comes. We will be caught up to meet him in the clouds. Two passages in the New Testament refer to this:

---

* **Assist News Service** - *www.assistnews.net*

Chapter 9 – The Great Tribulation

Matthew 24:36 "But about that day or hour no one knows, not even the angels in heaven, nor the Son, but only the Father. 37 As it was in the days of Noah, so it will be at the coming of the Son of Man. 38 For in the days before the flood, people were eating and drinking, marrying and giving in marriage, up to the day Noah entered the ark; 39 and they knew nothing about what would happen until the flood came and took them all away. That is how it will be <u>at the coming of the Son of Man. 40 Two men will be in the field; one will be taken and the other left. 41 Two women will be grinding with a hand mill; one will be taken and the other left</u>. 42 "Therefore keep watch, because you do not know on what day your Lord will come. 43 But understand this: If the owner of the house had known at what time of night the thief was coming, he would have kept watch and would not have let his house be broken into. 44 So you also must be ready, because the Son of Man will come at an hour when you do not expect him.

No-one will know the day or the hour when we will be *'taken up'*, will they? Why then does Yeshua instruct us to *'be ready'* and to *'keep watch'*? Those who are left will be taken by surprise. It will be a secret until it happens – just in the same way as the house-holder suddenly finding a thief in his house. But when it happens, the whole world will see and know!

1 Thessalonians 4:13 Brothers and sisters, we do not want you to be uninformed about those who sleep in death, so that you do not grieve like the rest of mankind, who have no hope. 14 For we believe that Jesus died and rose again, and so we believe that God will bring with Jesus those who have fallen asleep in him. 15 According to the Lord's word, we tell you that we who are still alive, who are left until the coming of the Lord, will certainly not precede those who have fallen asleep. 16 <u>For the Lord himself will come down from heaven, with a loud command, with the voice of the archangel and with the trumpet call of God, and the dead in Christ will rise first. 17 After that, we who are still alive and are left will be caught up together with them in the clouds to meet the Lord in the air.</u> And so we will be with the Lord forever. 18 Therefore encourage one another with these words.

These are certainly encouraging words and this event will definitely take place. The question is, *'When will it happen?'* When *'the Lord himself comes down from heaven, with a loud command, with the voice of the archangel and with the trumpet call of God.'*

Now, I don't know about you, but that doesn't sound like anything secret to me! Archangels voices tend to cause humans who hear them to tremble and fall down as if dead. (**Daniel 10:9,17, Ezekiel 1:26-28**) Also, the trumpet – and this is specifically the last trumpet – will sound loud and loonnggg!! Finally, as the Lord descends from heaven we are told:

> **Revelation 1:7** Look, <u>he is coming with the clouds, and every eye will see him</u>, even those who pierced him; and <u>all the peoples of the earth</u> will mourn because of him.

If *'all the peoples of the earth'* are going to witness his coming and mourn, then it won't be much of a secret, will it? It will take all of those people by surprise and they will be shocked and dismayed, but it will be an event witnessed by the whole world.

So, this event will NOT be a secret – though it *will* take most of the world by surprise (just as the fall of Mega-Babylon will!). However, if we pay attention to these writings of the prophets, then WE will not be taken by surprise.

The only question remaining is: WHEN will this take place? The clue is in that final trumpet sounding – when the *'dead in Christ* [the Messiah] *will rise first. <u>After that</u> ... we will be caught up.'* When does that final trumpet sound and the Messiah appear?

> **Revelation 10:1** Then I saw another mighty angel coming down from heaven. He was robed in a cloud, with a rainbow above his head; his face was like the sun, and his legs were like fiery pillars. 2 He was holding a little scroll, which lay open in his hand. He planted his right foot on the sea and his left foot on the land, 3 and <u>he gave a loud shout like the roar of a lion. When he shouted, the voices of the seven thunders spoke.</u> 4 And when the seven thunders spoke, I was about to write; but I heard a voice from heaven say, "Seal up what the seven thunders have said and do not

Chapter 9 – The Great Tribulation

write it down." 5 Then the angel I had seen standing on the sea and on the land raised his right hand to heaven. 6 And he swore by him who lives for ever and ever, who created the heavens and all that is in them, the earth and all that is in it, and the sea and all that is in it, and said, "<u>There will be no more delay! 7 But in the days when the seventh angel is about to sound his trumpet, the mystery of God will be accomplished</u>, just as he announced to his servants the prophets."

When, then, does this seventh trumpet sound and the Messiah take over?

> **Revelation 11:15** <u>The seventh angel sounded his trumpet</u>, and there were loud voices in heaven, which said: "<u>The kingdom of the world has become the kingdom of our Lord and of his Messiah, and he will reign for ever and ever</u>. 16 And the twenty-four elders, who were seated on their thrones before God, fell on their faces and worshiped God, 17 saying: "We give thanks to you, Lord God Almighty, the One who is and who was, because you have taken your great power and have begun to reign. 18 The nations were angry, <u>and your wrath has come</u>. The time has come for judging the dead, and for rewarding your servants the prophets and your people who revere your name, both great and small—and for destroying those who destroy the earth."

Note that when the seventh (last) trumpet sounds the elders say, *'Your wrath has come.'* This is the point when the Messiah will return and we will be caught up to meet the returning Yeshua and his angels.

> **1 Thessalonians 5:9** For God did not appoint us to suffer wrath but to receive salvation through our Lord Jesus Christ.

This passage comes immediately after the death of the two prophets in Jerusalem who, as we know, prophesied for the 1,260 days of the Great Tribulation. No, God has not appointed those who love Him to wrath, but we *will* have to endure the great tribulation.

Yeshua said, *"In this world you will have trouble (tribulation). But take heart! I have overcome the world."* (**John 16:33**)

> **Revelation 20:4** And I saw the souls of <u>those who had been beheaded because of their testimony about Jesus</u> and because of the word of God. They had not worshipped the

beast or its image and had not received its mark on their foreheads or their hands. They came to life and reigned with Christ a thousand years.

Matthew 24:29 Immediately <u>after the tribulation of those days shall the sun be darkened</u>, and the moon shall not give her light, and the stars shall fall from heaven, and the powers of the heavens shall be shaken:

A large number of our churches today – especially in the United States – believe and teach that we will not have to endure this time of trouble. We will escape out of it.

Well, we will be helped, that's for sure, but we are called to *'endure to the end.'* There is no guarantee that we will not suffer persecution – in fact, Yeshua promised the opposite!

Chapter 9 – The Great Tribulation

The Great Tribulation

1. In the middle of the last seven years (after the destruction of Babylon), the beast, Antichrist, will put a stop to the sacrifices in the Jewish temple and set up the *'abomination of desolation.'*

2. After subduing three of the ten rulers who gave him his power he will oppress the saints and change the set times and laws – for *'time, times and half a time.'*

3. His army will tramp on the holy city (Jerusalem) for 42 months.

4. Two prophets, clothed in sackcloth, will prophesy with great authority in Jerusalem for 1,260 days – and then be killed, to be resurrected 3½ days later.

5. Many of the Jewish people will be able to flee into the desert, to a place prepared by God for them, to be taken care of for 1,260 days, and again, for *'time, times and half a time.'*

6. The beast will exercise his authority for 42 months, to blaspheme God and to make war against the saints and conquer them.

7. *'There will be a time of distress such as has not happened from the beginning of nations until then,'* for *'time, times and half a time,'* i.e. Jacob's Trouble.

8. There <u>will be</u> a *'rapture'* event, being *'caught up into the clouds'*, but it will NOT be a secret – far from it! The whole earth – *'every eye'* – will witness it, when Jesus returns to rule his kingdom!

9. Our being *'caught up'* will take place at the seventh (last) trumpet, *after* the conclusion of the 1,260 days of the Great Tribulation!

10. When the seventh trumpet sounds the elders say, *'Your wrath has come'* – God's wrath will then be poured out on the unbelieving nations of the world.

10 – The mother of all battles

There is a hill in northern Israel, called Har Megiddo. It is the site of the ancient city of Megiddo, which has been excavated, and right next to it is a major junction between two main roads – the Jerusalem-Haifa road and the Tel Aviv-Tiberias road. Where these roads meet, in the middle of a large plain – known today as Megiddo Junction – is the site of the fabled *Armageddon!*

> **Revelation 16:12** The sixth angel poured out his bowl on the great river Euphrates, and its water was dried up <u>to prepare the way for the kings from the East</u>. 13 Then I saw three impure spirits that looked like frogs; they came out of the mouth of the dragon, out of the mouth of the beast and out of the mouth of the false prophet. 14 <u>They are demonic spirits that perform signs, and they go out to the kings of the whole world, to gather them for the battle on the great day of God Almighty</u>.
>
> 15 "Look, I come like a thief! Blessed is the one who stays awake and remains clothed, so as not to go naked and be shamefully exposed."
>
> 16 <u>Then they gathered the kings together to the place that in Hebrew is called Armageddon</u> (Har Megiddo).

We often hear people refer to the *'Battle of Armageddon'* as the ultimate battle. This WILL be the ultimate battle, but the title is misleading, because it is really the *Battle of Jerusalem*. This area beside Har Megiddo (Megiddo Junction) is simply a suitable assembly area for the armies planning to attack Jerusalem.

> **Zechariah 14:1** A day of YHWH is coming, Jerusalem, when your possessions will be plundered and divided up within your very walls. 2 <u>I will gather all the nations to Jerusalem to fight against it</u>; the city will be captured, the houses ransacked, and the women raped. Half of the city will go into exile, but the rest of the people will not be taken from the city. 3 <u>Then YHWH will go out and fight against those nations</u>, as he fights on a day of battle.

The Antichrist will gather all the nations of the world against Israel at Jerusalem. This will be his attempt to completely wipe out the – now greatly expanded – nation of Israel. Actually Zechariah says that it is YHWH himself who will gather all the nations – to contend with them there.

First, the wrath of God will be poured out upon the whole earth. This is probably what will incite all the nations to gather against Jerusalem.

> **Revelation 9:1** The fifth angel sounded his trumpet, and I saw a star that had fallen from the sky to the earth. The star was given the key to the shaft of the Abyss. 2 When he opened the Abyss, smoke rose from it like the smoke from a gigantic furnace. The sun and sky were darkened by the smoke from the Abyss. 3 And out of the smoke locusts came down on the earth and were given power like that of scorpions of the earth. 4 <u>They were told not to harm the grass of the earth or any plant or tree, but only those people who did not have the seal of God on their foreheads.</u> 5 They were not allowed to kill them but only to torture them for five months. And the agony they suffered was like that of the sting of a scorpion when it strikes. 6 During those days people will seek death but will not find it; they will long to die, but death will elude them. 7 The locusts looked like horses prepared for battle. On their heads they wore something like crowns of gold, and their faces resembled human faces. 8 Their hair was like women's hair, and their teeth were like lions' teeth. 9 They had breastplates like breastplates of iron, and the sound of their wings was like the thundering of many horses and chariots rushing into battle. 10 They had tails with stingers, like scorpions, and in their tails they had power to torment people for five months. 11 They had as king over them the angel of the Abyss, whose name in Hebrew is Abaddon and in Greek is Apollyon (that is, Destroyer).
>
> **Revelation 16:1** Then I heard a loud voice from the temple saying to the seven angels, "Go, pour out the seven bowls of God's wrath on the earth. 2 The first angel went and poured out his bowl on the land, and ugly, festering sores broke out on the people who had the mark of the beast and worshiped its image. 3 The second angel poured out his bowl on the sea, and it turned into blood like that of a dead person, and every living thing in the sea died. 4 The

Chapter 10 – The mother of all battles

third angel poured out his bowl on the rivers and springs of water, and they became blood. 5 Then I heard the angel in charge of the waters say: "You are just in these judgments, O Holy One, you who are and who were; 6 for they have shed the blood of your holy people and your prophets, and you have given them blood to drink as they deserve." 7 And I heard the altar respond: "Yes, Lord God Almighty, true and just are your judgments." 8 The fourth angel poured out his bowl on the sun, and the sun was allowed to scorch people with fire. 9 They were seared by the intense heat and they cursed the name of God, who had control over these plagues, but they refused to repent and glorify him. 10 The fifth angel poured out his bowl on the throne of the beast, and its kingdom was plunged into darkness. People gnawed their tongues in agony 11 and cursed the God of heaven because of their pains and their sores, but they refused to repent of what they had done.

This wrath of God is poured out upon all those who worship the beast and have received the mark of his name. It bears a striking resemblance to what happened to Egypt, when Pharaoh's heart was hardened and he refused to let the people of Israel go. The people of earth also harden their hearts and refuse to repent of their evil-doing and glorify Him.

This wrath is NOT for those who have refused that mark and who worship God alone and are being persecuted for that refusal. '*God did not appoint us to suffer wrath!*' (**1 Thessalonians 5:9**) and '*They were told ... to harm ... only those people who did not have the seal of God on their foreheads.*'

> **Revelation 16:12** The sixth angel poured out his bowl on the great river Euphrates, and its water was dried up to <u>prepare the way for the kings from the East.</u> 13 Then I saw three impure spirits that looked like frogs; they came out of the mouth of the dragon, out of the mouth of the beast and out of the mouth of the false prophet. 14 <u>They are demonic spirits that perform signs, and they go out to the kings of the whole world, to gather them for the battle on the great day of God Almighty.</u> 15 "Look, I come like a thief! Blessed is the one who stays awake and remains clothed, so as not to go naked and be shamefully exposed." 16 <u>Then they</u>

gathered the kings together to the place that in Hebrew is called Armageddon.

Revelation 9:13 The sixth angel sounded his trumpet, and I heard a voice coming from the four horns of the golden altar that is before God. 14 It said to the sixth angel who had the trumpet, "Release the four angels who are bound at the great river Euphrates." 15 And the four angels who had been kept ready for this very hour and day and month and year were released to kill a third of mankind. 16 The number of the mounted troops was twice ten thousand times ten thousand. I heard their number. 17 The horses and riders I saw in my vision looked like this: Their breastplates were fiery red, dark blue, and yellow as sulphur. The heads of the horses resembled the heads of lions, and out of their mouths came fire, smoke and sulphur. 18 A third of mankind was killed by the three plagues of fire, smoke and sulphur that came out of their mouths. 19 The power of the horses was in their mouths and in their tails; for their tails were like snakes, having heads with which they inflict injury. 20 The rest of mankind who were not killed by these plagues still did not repent of the work of their hands; they did not stop worshiping demons, and idols of gold, silver, bronze, stone and wood—idols that cannot see or hear or walk. 21 Nor did they repent of their murders, their magic arts, their sexual immorality or their thefts.

Now we can speculate on the nature of the weapons and armour described – it could be tanks, or other weapons – but how many nations could wield an army of 200 million men? These *"kings from the east"* must include China, which already boasts of its ability to field an army of 200 million soldiers.

All the nations of the earth will take part in this last stand against God and against Israel, because they recognise that He has His throne there:

Isaiah 29:5 But your many enemies will become like fine dust, the ruthless hordes like blown chaff. Suddenly, in an instant, 6 YHWH Almighty will come with thunder and earthquake and great noise, with whirlwind and tempest and flames of a devouring fire. 7 Then the hordes of all the nations that fight against Ariel, that attack her and her fortress and besiege her, will be as it is with a dream, with a vision in the

Chapter 10 – The mother of all battles

night – 8 as when a hungry person dreams of eating, but awakens hungry still; as when a thirsty person dreams of drinking, but awakens faint and thirsty still. <u>So will it be with the hordes of all the nations that fight against Mount Zion</u>. 9 Be stunned and amazed, blind yourselves and be sightless; be drunk, but not from wine, stagger, but not from beer. 10 YHWH has brought over you a deep sleep: he has sealed your eyes (the prophets); he has covered your heads (the seers).

Ezekiel 38:1 The word of YHWH came to me: 2 "Son of man, set your face against Gog, of the land of Magog, the chief prince of Meshek and Tubal; prophesy against him 3 and say: 'This is what the Sovereign YHWH says: I am against you, Gog, chief prince of Meshek and Tubal. 4 I will turn you around, put hooks in your jaws and bring you out with your whole army—your horses, your horsemen fully armed, and a great horde with large and small shields, all of them brandishing their swords. 5 Persia, Cush and Put will be with them, all with shields and helmets, 6 also Gomer with all its troops, and Beth Togarmah <u>from the far north with all its troops—the many nations with you</u>. 7 "'Get ready; be prepared, you and all the hordes gathered about you, and take command of them. 8 After many days you will be called to arms. In future years <u>you will invade a land that has recovered from war, whose people were gathered from many nations to the mountains of Israel, which had long been desolate. They had been brought out from the nations</u>, and now all of them live in safety. 9 You and all your troops <u>and the many nations with you will go up</u>, advancing like a storm; you will be like a cloud covering the land. 10 "'This is what the Sovereign YHWH says: On that day thoughts will come into your mind and you will devise an evil scheme. 11 You will say, "I will invade a land of unwalled villages; I will attack a peaceful and unsuspecting people—all of them living without walls and without gates and bars. 12 I will plunder and loot and turn my hand against the resettled ruins and the people gathered from the nations, rich in livestock and goods, living at the centre of the land [earth]." 13 Sheba and Dedan and the merchants of Tarshish and all her villages will say to you, "Have you come to plunder? Have you gathered your hordes to loot, to carry off silver and gold, to take away livestock and goods and to seize much plunder?"' 14 "Therefore, son of man, prophesy and say to Gog: 'This is what the Sovereign YHWH says: In that day, when my people Israel are living in safety, will you not take notice of it? 15 <u>You will come from your place in the far north, you and many nations with you, all of them riding on horses, a great horde, a mighty army</u>. 16 You will advance against my people Israel like a cloud that covers the land. In days to come, Gog, I will bring you against my land, so that the nations may know me when I am proved holy through you before their eyes.

17 "'This is what the Sovereign YHWH says: <u>You are the one I spoke of in former days by my servants the prophets of Israel.</u> At that time they prophesied for years that I would bring you against them. 18 This is what will happen in that day: When Gog attacks the land of Israel, my hot anger will be aroused, declares the Sovereign YHWH. 19 In my zeal and fiery wrath I declare that <u>at that time there shall be a great earthquake in the land of Israel.</u> 20 The fish in the sea, the birds in the sky, the beasts of the field, every creature that moves along the ground, and all the people on the face of the earth will tremble at my presence. The mountains will be overturned, the cliffs will crumble and every wall will fall to the ground. 21 I will summon a sword against Gog on all my mountains, declares the Sovereign YHWH. Every man's sword will be against his brother. 22 <u>I will execute judgment on him with plague and bloodshed; I will pour down torrents of rain, hailstones and burning sulphur on him and on his troops and on the many nations with him</u>. 23 And so I will show my greatness and my holiness, and I will make myself known in the sight of many nations. Then they will know that I am YHWH.'

Zechariah 14:1 A day of YHWH is coming, Jerusalem, when your possessions will be plundered and divided up within your very walls. 2 <u>I will gather all the nations to Jerusalem to fight against it</u>; the city will be captured, the houses ransacked, and the women raped. Half of the city will go into exile, but the rest of the people will not be taken from the city.

Isaiah 34:34 Come near, you nations, and listen; pay attention, you peoples! Let the earth hear, and all that is in it, the world, and all that comes out of it! 2 <u>YHWH is angry with all nations; his wrath is on all their armies. He will totally destroy them, he will give them over to slaughter.</u> 3 Their slain will be thrown out, their dead bodies will stink; the

Chapter 10 — The mother of all battles

mountains will be soaked with their blood. 4 All the stars in the sky will be dissolved and the heavens rolled up like a scroll; all the starry host will fall like withered leaves from the vine, like shrivelled figs from the fig-tree.

A place called Armageddon

1 Actually, Har Megiddo, an ancient hill fortress in northern Israel, close to the junction of the two major north-south trade routes and a suitable gathering place for armies coming from the north to attack Jerusalem.

2 This is not the battle of Armageddon, but the Battle for Jerusalem – Armageddon is simply where the Antichrist, with the armies of all the nations, will assemble before attacking Jerusalem.

3 God's wrath will be poured out upon the nations ruled by the *antichrist* in the form of many plagues – stirring them to an angry response against Israel.

4 '*Demonic spirits that perform signs,* [will] *go out to the kings of the whole world, to gather them for the battle on the great day of God Almighty.*'

5 The *'kings of the east'* will field an army of 200 million men, armed with powerful weapons.

6 They '*will advance against ... Israel like a cloud that covers the land.*'

11 – The end of the Beast

In the first chapter of the Book of Acts the disciples witness Yeshua ascending into heaven:

> **Acts 1:6** Then they gathered around him and asked him, "Lord, are you at this time going to restore the kingdom to Israel?" 7 He said to them: "It is not for you to know the times or dates the Father has set by his own authority. 8 But you will receive power when the Holy Spirit comes on you; and you will be my witnesses in Jerusalem, and in all Judea and Samaria, and to the ends of the earth." 9 <u>After he said this, he was taken up before their very eyes, and a cloud hid him from their sight</u>. 10 They were looking intently up into the sky as he was going, when suddenly two men dressed in white stood beside them. 11 "Men of Galilee," they said, "why do you stand here looking into the sky? <u>This same Jesus, who has been taken from you into heaven, will come back in the same way you have seen him go into heaven.</u>"

These two angels declare that Jesus will return to earth in the same way that he left. He will come in the clouds (accompanied by his saints gathered up from the four corners of the earth, plus his holy angels) and descend to the Mount of Olives.

When Yeshua returns to the Mount of Olives – as promised in **Zechariah 14:3** and **Acts 1:9-11**, above – he will then personally enter into battle with the antichrist and the armies of all the nations (200 million troops from the *'kings of the east'* alone!). And he will not be alone! He will be accompanied by a host of angels and by us, his resurrected followers:

> **Matthew 25:31** 'When the Son of Man comes in his glory, <u>and all the angels with him</u>, he will sit on his glorious throne.

> **2 Thessalonians 1:7** <u>when the Lord Jesus is revealed from heaven in blazing fire with his powerful angels. 8 He will punish those who do not know God</u> and do not obey the gospel of our Lord Jesus. 9 They will be punished with everlasting destruction and shut out from the presence of the

Lord and from the glory of his might 10 on the day he comes <u>to be glorified in his holy people and to be marvelled at among all those who have believed. This includes you</u>, because you believed our testimony to you.

1 Thessalonians 3:13 May he strengthen your hearts so that you will be blameless and holy in the presence of our God and Father <u>when our Lord Jesus comes with all his holy ones</u>.

Psalm 98:9 let them sing before the Lord, for <u>he comes to judge the earth</u>. He will judge the world in righteousness and the peoples with equity.

Isaiah 30:27 See, <u>the Name of YHWH comes from afar, with burning anger</u> and dense clouds of smoke; his lips are full of wrath, <u>and his tongue is a consuming fire</u>.

Isaiah 40:10 See, <u>the Sovereign YHWH comes with power, and he rules with a mighty arm. See</u>, his reward is with him, and <u>his recompense accompanies him</u>.

Isaiah 62:11 YHWH has made proclamation to the ends of the earth: 'Say to Daughter Zion, "<u>See, your Saviour comes! See</u>, his reward is with him, and h<u>is recompense accompanies him</u>."'

Zechariah 14:3 Then <u>YHWH will go out and fight against those nations, as he fights on a day of battle. 4 On that day his feet will stand on the Mount of Olives</u>, east of Jerusalem, and the Mount of Olives will be split in two from east to west, ... Then <u>YHWH my God will come, and all the holy ones with him</u>.

Micah 1:3 Look! <u>YHWH is coming from his dwelling-place; he comes down and treads on the heights of the earth. 4 The mountains melt beneath him and the valleys split apart</u>, like wax before the fire, like water rushing down a slope.

Isaiah 41:25 'I have stirred up one from the north, and <u>he comes – one from the rising sun who calls on my name. He treads on rulers as if they were mortar, as if he were a potter treading the clay</u>.

26 Who told of this from the beginning, so that we could know, or beforehand, so that we could say, "He was right"? No one told of this, no one foretold it, no one heard any words from you. 27 I was the first to tell Zion, "Look, here they are!" I gave to Jerusalem a messenger of good news.

Chapter 11 – The end of the Beast

28 I look but there is no one – no one among the gods to give counsel, no one to give answer when I ask them. 29 See, they are all false! Their deeds amount to nothing; their images are but wind and confusion.

Daniel 7:13 "In my vision at night I looked, and <u>there before me was one like a son of man, coming with the clouds of heaven</u>. He approached the Ancient of Days and was led into his presence. 14 He was given authority, glory and sovereign power; <u>all nations and peoples of every language worshipped him</u>. His dominion is an everlasting dominion that will not pass away, and his kingdom is one that will never be destroyed.

The same passage in Zechariah – where we read previously of the invasion of Jerusalem – continues:

Zechariah 14:3 Then YHWH will go out and fight against those nations, as he fights on a day of battle. 4 <u>On that day his feet will stand on the Mount of Olives, east of Jerusalem, and the Mount of Olives will be split in two from east to west, forming a great valley, with half of the mountain moving north and half moving south</u>. ...

5 Then <u>YHWH my God will come, and all the holy ones with him</u>. 6 On that day there will be neither sunlight nor cold, frosty darkness. 7 It will be a unique day—a day known only to YHWH—with no distinction between day and night. When evening comes, there will be light. 8 On that day living water will flow out from Jerusalem, half of it east to the Dead Sea and half of it west to the Mediterranean Sea, in summer and in winter. 9 <u>YHWH will be king over the whole earth. On that day there will be one YHWH, and his name the only name</u>.

Isaiah 33:10 'Now will I arise,' says YHWH. '<u>Now will I be exalted; now will I be lifted up</u>. 11 You conceive chaff, you give birth to straw; your breath is a fire that consumes you. 12 <u>The peoples will be burned to ashes; like cut thorn-bushes they will be set ablaze</u>.' 23 Then <u>an abundance of spoils will be divided and even the lame will carry off plunder</u>. 24 No one living in Zion will say, 'I am ill'; and the sins of those who dwell there will be forgiven.

The book of Revelation backs this up:

Revelation 10:1 Then I saw another mighty angel coming down from heaven. He was robed in a cloud, with a rainbow above his head; his face was like the sun, and his legs were like fiery pillars. 2 He was holding a little scroll, which lay open in his hand. He planted his right foot on the sea and his left foot on the land, 3 and he gave a loud shout like the roar of a lion. When he shouted, the voices of the seven thunders spoke. 4 And when the seven thunders spoke, I was about to write; but I heard a voice from heaven say, "Seal up what the seven thunders have said and do not write it down." 5 Then the angel I had seen standing on the sea and on the land raised his right hand to heaven. 6 And he swore by him who lives for ever and ever, who created the heavens and all that is in them, the earth and all that is in it, and the sea and all that is in it, and said, <u>"There will be no more delay! 7 But in the days when the seventh angel is about to sound his trumpet, the mystery of God will be accomplished, just as he announced to his servants the prophets."</u>

Revelation 11:15 The seventh angel sounded his trumpet, and there were loud voices in heaven, which said: "The kingdom of the world has become the kingdom of our Lord and of his Messiah, and he will reign for ever and ever.

Revelation 16:17 The seventh angel poured out his bowl into the air, and out of the temple came a loud voice from the throne, saying, "It is done!" 18 Then there came flashes of lightning, rumblings, peals of thunder and <u>a severe earthquake. No earthquake like it has ever occurred since mankind has been on earth, so tremendous was the quake. 19 The great city split into three parts, and the cities of the nations collapsed.</u> God remembered Babylon the Great and gave her the cup filled with the wine of the fury of his wrath. 20 Every island fled away and the mountains could not be found. 21 <u>From the sky huge hailstones, each weighing about a hundred pounds, fell on people. And they cursed God on account of the plague of hail, because the plague was so terrible.</u>

When the seventh angel sounds his trumpet, it is the end. Yeshua himself will appear in the clouds, accompanied by his armies and will destroy the forces of the nations who are fighting against Israel. As his foot descends once again onto the Mount of Olives, there will be a tremendous earthquake – which will change the face of all the land around Jerusalem.

Revelation 16:18 Then <u>there came ... a severe earthquake. No earthquake like it has ever occurred since mankind has been on earth, so tremendous was the quake. 19</u>

Chapter 11 – The end of the Beast

The great city split into three parts, and the cities of the nations collapsed.

Isaiah 29:5 But your many enemies will become like fine dust, the ruthless hordes like blown chaff. Suddenly, in an instant, 6 YHWH Almighty will come with thunder and earthquake and great noise, with whirlwind and tempest and flames of a devouring fire. 7 Then the hordes of all the nations that fight against Ariel, that attack her and her fortress and besiege her, will be as it is with a dream, with a vision in the night.

Ezekiel 38:18 This is what will happen in that day: when Gog attacks the land of Israel, my hot anger will be aroused, declares the Sovereign YHWH. 19 In my zeal and fiery wrath I declare that at that time there shall be a great earthquake in the land of Israel. 20 The fish in the sea, the birds in the sky, the beasts of the field, every creature that moves along the ground, and all the people on the face of the earth will tremble at my presence. The mountains will be overturned, the cliffs will crumble and every wall will fall to the ground.

This will be the greatest earthquake ever seen – *'No earthquake like it has ever occurred since mankind has been on earth.'* Jerusalem will *'split into three parts,' 'the cities of the nations collapsed,' 'every island fled away and the mountains could not be found,' 'the mountains will be overturned, the cliffs will crumble and every wall will fall to the ground.'*

This earthquake at Yeshua's return will change the whole landscape of Jerusalem:

Zechariah 14:10 The whole land, from Geba to Rimmon, south of Jerusalem, will become like the Arabah. But Jerusalem will be raised up high from the Benjamin Gate to the site of the First Gate, to the Corner Gate, and from the Tower of Hananel to the royal winepresses, and will remain in its place. 11 It will be inhabited; never again will it be destroyed. Jerusalem will be secure.

Revelation 19:11 I saw heaven standing open and there before me was a white horse, whose rider is called Faithful and True. With justice he judges and wages war. 12 His eyes are like blazing fire, and on his head are many crowns. He has a name written on him that no one knows but he himself. 13 He is dressed in a robe dipped in blood, and his name is the Word of God. 14 The armies of heaven were following him, riding on white horses and dressed in fine linen, white and clean. 15 Coming out of his mouth is a sharp sword with which to strike down the nations. "He will rule them with an iron sceptre." He treads the winepress of the fury of the wrath of God Almighty. 16 On his robe and on his thigh he has this name written: KING OF KINGS AND LORD OF LORDS.

Who are the ones dressed in fine linen – not the angels, but the resurrected saints!

2 Thessalonians 2:8 And then the lawless one will be revealed, whom the Lord Jesus will overthrow with the breath of his mouth and destroy by the splendour of his coming.

Malachi 4:1 'Surely the day is coming; it will burn like a furnace. All the arrogant and every evildoer will be stubble, and that day that is coming will set them on fire,' says YHWH Almighty. 'Not a root or a branch will be left to them. 2 But for you who revere my name, the sun of righteousness will rise with healing in its rays. And you will go out and frolic like well-fed calves. 3 Then you will trample on the wicked; they will be ashes under the soles of your feet on the day when I act,' says YHWH Almighty.

Who will trample on the wicked? *'You who revere my name ... you will go out ... you will trample on the wicked; they will be ashes under the soles of your feet!'*, says Malachi. The army of God is described in more detail in Joel:

Joel 2:1 Blow the trumpet in Zion; sound the alarm on my holy hill. Let all who live in the land tremble, for the day of YHWH is coming. It is close at hand – 2 a day of darkness and gloom, a day of clouds and blackness. Like dawn spreading across the mountains a large and mighty army comes, such as never was in ancient times nor ever will be in ages to come. 3 Before them fire devours, behind them a flame blazes. Before them the land is like the garden of Eden, behind them, a desert waste – nothing escapes them. 4 They have the appearance of horses; they gallop along like cavalry. 5 With a noise like that of chariots they leap over the mountain-tops, like a crackling fire consuming stubble, like a mighty army drawn up for battle. 6 At the sight of them, nations are in anguish; every face turns pale. 7 They charge like warriors; they scale walls like soldiers. They all march in line, not swerving from their course. 8 They do not jostle each other; each marches straight ahead. They plunge through defences without breaking ranks. 9 They rush upon the city; they run along the wall.

Chapter 11 – The end of the Beast

They climb into the houses; like thieves they enter through the windows. 10 Before them the earth shakes, the heavens tremble, the sun and moon are darkened, and the stars no longer shine. 11 <u>YHWH thunders at the head of his army; his forces are beyond number</u>, and mighty is the army that obeys his command. T<u>he day of YHWH is great; it is dreadful</u>. Who can endure it?

Zechariah carries on to describe the destruction of the armies of all the nations:

Zechariah 14:12 This is the plague with which YHWH will strike all the nations that fought against Jerusalem: <u>Their flesh will rot while they are still standing on their feet, their eyes will rot in their sockets, and their tongues will rot in their mouths</u>. 13 On that day people will be stricken by YHWH with great panic. They will seize each other by the hand and attack one another. 14 <u>Judah too will fight</u> at Jerusalem. <u>The wealth of all the surrounding nations will be collected—great quantities of gold and silver and clothing</u>. 15 A similar plague will strike the horses and mules, the camels and donkeys, and all the animals in those camps.

The armies gathered against Jerusalem will experience something akin to a nuclear holocaust – whether <u>actual</u> nuclear weapons, or a supernatural flash, we don't know. They will also panic and attack one another – something which has happened many times when enemies have come against Israel. Israel also will fight and overcome them.

Revelation 19:17 And I saw an angel standing in the sun, who cried in a loud voice to all the birds flying in midair, "Come, gather together for the great supper of God, 18 so that you may eat the flesh of kings, generals, and the mighty, of horses and their riders, and the flesh of all people, free and slave, great and small." 19 Then I saw <u>the beast and the kings of the earth and their armies gathered together to wage war against the rider on the horse and his army</u>. 20 But the beast was captured, and with it the false prophet who had performed the signs on its behalf. With these signs he had deluded those who had received the mark of the beast and worshiped its image. The two of them were thrown alive into the fiery lake of burning sulfur. 21 The rest were killed with the sword coming out of the mouth of the rider on the horse, and all the birds gorged themselves on their flesh.

The Lord gave Ezekiel a very similar picture of this. Once again the kings of the earth and their armies are described as food for the birds and wild animals.

Ezekiel 39:17 "Son of man, this is what the Sovereign YHWH says: Call out to every kind of bird and all the wild animals: 'Assemble and come together from all around to the sacrifice I am preparing for you, the great sacrifice on the mountains of Israel. There you will eat flesh and drink blood. 18 You will eat the flesh of mighty men and drink the blood of the princes of the earth as if they were rams and lambs, goats and bulls—all of them fattened animals from Bashan. 19 At the sacrifice I am preparing for you, you will eat fat till you are glutted and drink blood till you are drunk. 20 At my table you will eat your fill of horses and riders, mighty men and soldiers of every kind,' declares the Sovereign YHWH.

Earlier in the same chapter he says:

Ezekiel 38:1 "Son of man, prophesy against Gog and say: 'This is what the Sovereign YHWH says: I am against you, Gog, chief prince of Meshek and Tubal. 2 I will turn you around and drag you along. I will bring you from the far north and send you against the mountains of Israel. 3 Then I will strike your bow from your left hand and make your arrows drop from your right hand. 4 <u>On the mountains of Israel you will fall, you and all your troops and the nations with you</u>. I will give you as food to all kinds of carrion birds and to the wild animals. 5 You will fall in the open field, for I have spoken, declares the Sovereign YHWH. 6 I will send fire on Magog and on those who live in safety in the coastlands, and they will know that I am YHWH.

7 "'I will make known my holy name among my people Israel. I will no longer let my holy name be profaned, and the nations will know that I YHWH am the Holy One in Israel. 8 It is coming! It will surely take place, declares the Sovereign YHWH. <u>This is the day I have spoken of</u>.

9 "'Then those who live in the towns of Israel will go out and use the weapons for fuel and burn them up—the small and large shields, the bows and arrows, the war clubs and spears. For seven years they will use them for fuel. 10 They

will not need to gather wood from the fields or cut it from the forests, because they will use the weapons for fuel. And they will plunder those who plundered them and loot those who looted them, declares the Sovereign YHWH.

There will be so many discarded weapons, not required for war anymore, so they will be used as fuel – and will last for seven years!

> 11 "'On that day I will give Gog a burial place in Israel, in the valley of those who travel east of the Sea. It will block the way of travellers, because Gog and all his hordes will be buried there. So it will be called the Valley of Hamon Gog. (the hordes of Gog) 12 "'For seven months the Israelites will be burying them in order to cleanse the land. 13 All the people of the land will bury them, and the day I display my glory will be a memorable day for them, declares the Sovereign YHWH. 14 People will be continually employed in cleansing the land. They will spread out across the land and, along with others, they will bury any bodies that are lying on the ground. "'After the seven months they will carry out a more detailed search. 15 As they go through the land, anyone who sees a human bone will leave a marker beside it until the gravediggers bury it in the Valley of Hamon Gog, 16 near a town called Hamonah. And so they will cleanse the land.'

As we can see the practical clearing up operation after this battle will be a major undertaking. But what does it mean that the Messiah has returned to earth to reign? What will his kingdom be like?

The Return of the King

1 When, after his resurrection, Yeshua ascended into the clouds from the Mount of Olives, the angel promised that he would return in just the same way.

2 Daniel says he will come with the clouds of heaven and all nations will worship him. His kingdom will last forever.

3 Zechariah supports this by describing His feet touching the Mount of Olives, instigating a tremendous earthquake which will split the mountain in two, east-west. A river will flow

out of the city in two different directions: east to the Dead Sea and west to the Mediterranean Sea.

4 According to Revelation, this earthquake will have repercussions around the whole earth, causing the cities of the nations to collapse!

5 The Messiah will appear accompanied by his armies, including the righteous from all over the earth and those who have died, now resurrected.

6 He (and we) will go to battle against the Antichrist beast and all the rulers and armies of the earth – destroying them with *"the brightness of his coming."*

7 The armies will be destroyed by a plague similar to a nuclear attack. In addition, they will turn in panic and attack one another, as well as being attacked by Israel and the armies of God (his resurrected saints).

8 Their bodies will be eaten by the birds and wild beasts upon the mountains of Israel and it will take at least seven months to bury all the remains.

9 The discarded weapons will be collected up by Israel and used as fuel for seven years – being no longer required for defence.

10 The thousand year reign of the Messiah has begun!

12 – Millennium reign of Messiah

The Messiah has come at last to reign on earth and his first action – apart from gathering his followers from the four corners of the earth and resurrecting those *"fallen asleep"* – is to war against the Antichrist and the armies of all the nations of the world.

Their armies are now gone – completely wiped out, and buried on the mountains of Israel, but those nations themselves still remain. They received the *"mark of the beast"* and worshipped him – hating the Messiah and his followers – yet many of them (though not all) are still alive and have been spared.

Resurrected, or caught up to meet him

Those who love the Messiah will either have been resurrected at his appearance or – those who are still alive – caught up to meet Him in the clouds. As Paul tells us:

> **1 Corinthians 15:51** Listen, I tell you a mystery: <u>We will not all sleep, but we will all be changed— 52 in a flash, in the twinkling of an eye, at the last trumpet. For the trumpet will sound, the dead will be raised imperishable, and we will be changed</u>. 53 For the perishable must clothe itself with the imperishable, and the mortal with immortality. 54 When the perishable has been clothed with the imperishable, and the mortal with immortality, then the saying that is written will come true: "Death has been swallowed up in victory."

All of Messiah's followers will be changed from having mortal bodies, to immortal ones. We will *"be like the angels in heaven,"* Yeshua says in **Matthew 22:30**. This will not be the case for the surviving people of the nations around the world, who have just spent the last 3½ years hating God, his Messiah and those who follow him.

Messiah's Wedding and Award Ceremony

When the Messiah comes, he will *"present [the church] to himself, as a radiant church, without stain or wrinkle or any other blemish, but holy and blameless."* (**Ephesians 5:25**) He will celebrate a wedding feast, with the church as his bride:

Matthew 25:10 The bridegroom arrived. The virgins who were ready went in with him to the wedding banquet. And the door was shut.

Revelation 21:9 "Come, I will show you the bride, the wife of the Lamb." 10 And he carried me away in the Spirit to a mountain great and high, and showed me the Holy City, Jerusalem, coming down out of heaven from God. 11 It shone with the glory of God, and its brilliance was like that of a very precious jewel, like a jasper, clear as crystal.

He will begin his reign by what is commonly referred to as *"the judgement seat of Christ (Messiah)"*.

Romans 14:10 For we will all stand before God's judgment seat.

2 Corinthians 5:10 For we must all appear before the judgment seat of Christ, that each one may receive what is due him for the things done while in the body, whether good or bad.

Revelation 11:18 The time has come for judging the dead, and for rewarding your servants the prophets and your people who revere your name, both great and small."

This is not a judgement seat as in a courtroom (which will come at the end of the millennium), but more like an award ceremony at the end of an athletic contest, where the trophies are awarded for achievement.

Luke 14:12 Then Jesus said to his host, "When you give a luncheon or dinner, do not invite your friends, your brothers or relatives, or your rich neighbors; if you do, they may invite you back and so you will be repaid. 13 But when you give a banquet, invite the poor, the crippled, the lame, the blind, 14 and you will be blessed. Although they cannot repay you, you will be repaid at the resurrection of the righteous."

Mark 10:21 Jesus looked at him and loved him. "One thing you lack," he said. "Go, sell everything you have and give to the poor, <u>and you will have treasure in heaven</u>. Then come, follow me."

Luke 12:33 Sell your possessions and give to the poor. <u>Provide purses for yourselves that will not wear out, a treasure in heaven that will not be exhausted</u>, where no thief comes near and no moth destroys.

Luke 19:15 "He was made king, however, and returned home. Then he sent for the servants to whom he had given the money, in order to find out what they had gained with it. 16 "The first one came and said, 'Sir, your mina has earned ten more.' 17 "'Well done, my good servant!' his master replied. 'Because <u>you have been trustworthy in a very small matter, take charge of ten cities</u>.' 18 "The second came and said, 'Sir, your mina has earned five more.' 19 "<u>His master answered, 'You take charge of five cities</u>.'

Those who follow Yeshua will be judged by the deeds he/she has done while alive, *"in the body."* They will receive rewards according to their faithfulness, as Yeshua stated in the parable above. Those rewards will include responsibility for governing the nations of the world – ruling over cities!

Revelation 19:6 Then I heard what sounded like a great multitude, like the roar of rushing waters and like loud peals of thunder, shouting: "Hallelujah! For our Lord God Almighty reigns. 7 Let us rejoice and be glad and give him glory! For <u>the wedding of the Lamb has come, and his bride has made herself ready</u>. 8 Fine linen, bright and clean, was given her to wear." (Fine linen stands for the righteous acts of the saints.) 9 Then the angel said to me, "Write: 'Blessed are those who are invited to <u>the wedding supper of the Lamb</u>!'"

This award ceremony will include the great *"Wedding Feast of the Lamb":*

<u>Ruling the nations with a rod of iron</u>

The Messiah has returned to *'rule the nations with a rod of iron.'*

Psalm 2:9 <u>You will rule them with an iron sceptre</u>; you will dash them to pieces like pottery."

Psalm 110:2 YHWH will extend your mighty sceptre from Zion; <u>you will rule in the midst of your enemies</u>.

Revelation 2:27 <u>He will rule them with an iron sceptre;</u> he will dash them to pieces like pottery' – just as I have received authority from my Father.

Revelation 12:5 She gave birth to a son, <u>a male child, who will rule all the nations with an iron sceptre</u>. And her child was snatched up to God and to his throne.

Revelation 19:15 Out of his mouth comes a sharp sword with which to strike down the nations. "<u>He will rule them with an iron sceptre.</u>" He treads the winepress of the fury of the wrath of God Almighty.

Isaiah 45:23 By myself I have sworn, my mouth has uttered in all integrity a word that will not be revoked: Before me every knee will bow; by me every tongue will swear.

Romans 14:11 It is written: "'As surely as I live,' says the Lord, '<u>every knee will bow before me; every tongue will confess to God.</u>'"

Phillippians 2:10 that <u>at the name of Jesus every knee should bow</u>, in heaven and on earth and under the earth,

Zechariah 14:16 Then the survivors from <u>all the nations that have attacked Jerusalem will go up year after year to worship the King, YHWH Almighty, and to celebrate the Festival of Tabernacles.</u> 17 If any of the peoples of the earth do not go up to Jerusalem to worship the King, YHWH Almighty, they will have no rain. 18 If the Egyptian people do not go up and take part, they will have no rain. YHWH will bring on them the plague he inflicts on the nations that do not go up to celebrate the Festival of Tabernacles. 19 This will be the punishment of Egypt and the punishment of all the nations that do not go up to celebrate the Festival of Tabernacles.

We shall reign with Him

Not only will the Messiah reign over the whole earth, but his faithful followers will reign with Him. This was the import of all those parables Yeshua taught, about ruling over 10 cities, etc.

2 Timothy 2:12 If we endure, <u>we will also reign with him</u>.

Revelation 20:1 And I saw an angel coming down out of heaven, having the key to the Abyss and holding in his hand a

Chapter 12 – Millennium reign of Messiah

great chain. 2 <u>He seized the dragon, that ancient serpent, who is the devil, or Satan, and bound him for a thousand years.</u> 3 He threw him into the Abyss, and locked and sealed it over him, to keep him from deceiving the nations anymore <u>until the thousand years were ended</u>. After that, he must be set free for a short time.

4 I saw thrones on which were seated those who had been given authority to judge. And I saw the souls of those who had been beheaded because of their testimony for Jesus and because of the word of God. They had not worshiped the beast or his image and had not received his mark on their foreheads or their hands. <u>They came to life and reigned with Christ a thousand years</u>. 5 (The rest of the dead did not come to life until the thousand years were ended.) This is the first resurrection. 6 Blessed and holy are those who have part in the first resurrection. The second death has no power over them, but <u>they will be priests of God and of Christ and will reign with him for a thousand years</u>.

Those we will reign over will be reluctant subjects – although probably relieved also to be out from under the oppressive reign of the antichrist. This reign will be administered from Jerusalem, where the Messiah will set up his throne:

Zechariah 14:20 On that day HOLY TO YHWH will be inscribed on the bells of the horses, and the cooking pots in YHWH's house will be like the sacred bowls in front of the altar. 21 Every pot in Jerusalem and Judah will be holy to YHWH Almighty, and <u>all who come to sacrifice</u> will take some of the pots and cook in them. And on that day there will no longer be a Canaanite in the house of YHWH Almighty.

The River of Life

There will be great physical changes on the earth, especially around Jerusalem. We have mentioned the great earthquake which will split the Mount of Olives as the Messiah's foot touches it.

Zechariah 14:8 <u>On that day living water will flow out from Jerusalem, half to the eastern sea and half to the western sea</u>, in summer and in winter. 9 YHWH will be king over the whole earth. On that day there will be one YHWH, and his name the only name.

Under the temple site, in the City of David, is the Gihon spring — which is a syphon spring, in other words the water gushes out under pressure. It looks like the changes in the topography after the great earthquake will cause this spring to flow out in two directions in future.

Revelation 22:1 Then the angel showed me <u>the river of the water of life, as clear as crystal, flowing from the throne of God and of the Lamb 2 down the middle of the great street of the city</u>. On each side of the river stood the tree of life, bearing twelve crops of fruit, yielding its fruit every month. <u>And the leaves of the tree are for the healing of the nations</u>.

The river of living water flows into the Dead Sea, bringing it to life — the water will become fresh, teeming with fish:

Ezekiel 47:1 The man brought me back to the entrance of the temple, <u>and I saw water coming out from under the threshold of the temple toward the east</u> (for the temple faced east). The water was coming down from under the south side of the temple, south of the altar. 2 He then brought me out through the north gate and led me around the outside to the outer gate facing east, and the water was flowing from the south side.

6 Then he led me back to the bank of the river. 7 When I arrived there, I saw a great number of trees on each side of the river. 8 He said to me, "This water flows toward the eastern region and goes down into the Arabah, where it enters the [Dead] Sea. <u>When it empties into the Sea, the water there becomes fresh. 9 Swarms of living creatures will live wherever the river flows. There will be large numbers of fish, because this water flows there and makes the salt water fresh; so where the river flows everything will live</u>. 10 Fishermen will stand along the shore; from En Gedi to En Eglaim there will be places for spreading nets. The fish will be of many kinds—like the fish of the Great Sea [Mediterranean]. 11 But the swamps and marshes will not become fresh; they will be left for salt. 12 <u>Fruit trees of all kinds will grow on both banks of the river.</u> Their leaves will not wither, nor will their fruit fail. Every month they will bear, because the water from the sanctuary flows to them. <u>Their fruit will serve for food and their leaves for healing</u>."

The trees growing beside this river will produce both fruit and leaves that bring healing to the nations.

Chapter 12 – Millennium reign of Messiah

The Final Judgement

During this 1,000 year reign, Satan has been bound and is unable to deceive the nations of the world. There will be 1,000 years of peace, healing and righteous rule by the Messiah and his followers.

> **Revelation 20:1** And I saw an angel coming down out of heaven, having the key to the Abyss and holding in his hand a great chain. 2 <u>He seized the dragon, that ancient serpent, who is the devil, or Satan, and bound him for a thousand years.</u> 3 He threw him into the Abyss, and locked and sealed it over him, to keep him from deceiving the nations anymore <u>until the thousand years were ended</u>. After that, he must be set free for a short time.

At the end of the millennium, the nations of the earth are tested by Satan one last time:

> **Revelation 20:7** <u>When the thousand years are over, Satan will be released from his prison 8 and will go out to deceive the nations in the four corners of the earth</u>—Gog and Magog—to gather them for battle. In number they are like the sand on the seashore. 9 They marched across the breadth of the earth and surrounded the camp of God's people, the city he loves. <u>But fire came down from heaven and devoured them</u>. 10 And the devil, who deceived them, was thrown into the lake of burning sulfur, where the beast and the false prophet had been thrown. They will be tormented day and night for ever and ever.

Even after 1,000 years of righteousness and peace, the nations of the earth will allow themselves to be deceived once again and will come in battle against the Messiah and God's people.

> **Daniel 7:9** "As I looked, "<u>thrones were set in place, and the Ancient of Days took his seat</u>. His clothing was as white as snow; the hair of his head was white like wool. His throne was flaming with fire, and its wheels were all ablaze. 10 A river of fire was flowing, coming out from before him. Thousands upon thousands attended him; ten thousand times ten thousand stood before him. <u>The court was seated, and the books were opened</u>.

Revelation 20:11 Then <u>I saw a great white throne and him who was seated on it</u>. Earth and sky fled from his presence, and there was no place for them. 12 And I saw the dead, great and small, standing before the throne, <u>and books were opened. Another book was opened, which is the book of life. The dead were judged according to what they had done as recorded in the books</u>. 13 The sea gave up the dead that were in it, and death and Hades gave up the dead that were in them, and each person was judged according to what he had done. 14 Then death and Hades were thrown into the lake of fire. The lake of fire is the second death. 15 <u>If anyone's name was not found written in the book of life, he was thrown into the lake of fire</u>.

A New Heaven and a New Earth

Revelation 21:1 Then I saw "a new heaven and a new earth," for the first heaven and the first earth had passed away, and there was no longer any sea. 2 I saw the Holy City, the new Jerusalem, coming down out of heaven from God, prepared as a bride beautifully dressed for her husband. 3 And I heard a loud voice from the throne saying, "Look! God's dwelling place is now among the people, and he will dwell with them. They will be his people, and God himself will be with them and be their God. 4 '<u>He will wipe every tear from their eyes. There will be no more death</u>' or <u>mourning or crying or pain</u>, for the old order of things has passed away."

5 He who was seated on the throne said, "I am making everything new!" Then he said, "Write this down, for these words are trustworthy and true." 6 He said to me: "It is done. I am the Alpha and the Omega, the Beginning and the End. To the thirsty I will give water without cost from the spring of the water of life. 7 Those who are victorious will inherit all this, and I will be their God and they will be my children.

8 But the cowardly, the unbelieving, the vile, the murderers, the sexually immoral, those who practice magic arts, the idolaters and all liars—they will be consigned to the fiery lake of burning sulphur. This is the second death."

Chapter 12 – Millennium reign of Messiah

The Millennium

1. The 1,000 years will begin when the Messiah's foot touches the Mount of Olives in Jerusalem.

2. Before he arrives, he will gather all of his people, dead and those still alive (the first resurrection), from the four corners of the earth. We will all be changed *'in the twinkling of an eye'* into immortal bodies, and we will accompany him as he arrives.

3. The Messiah will go to war and totally wipe out all those armies (millions of men), from all of the nations, who have assembled against him.

4. He will present his bride (his followers, the *'body of Messiah'*) to himself, *'pure and spotless, without wrinkle or blemish'* and celebrate a great *'wedding feast of the Lamb'* with his people.

5. As part of this he will host an award ceremony, the *'judgement seat of Christ,'* where the faithful will be rewarded for what they have done. Some will be made rulers over several cities, some over a few – depending on what *'treasure in heaven'* they stored up while on earth.

6. He will rule over the survivors of the nations of the world with a *'rod of iron'* and we will rule with him.

7. Jerusalem will be the capital of the earth, raised up with all the land flat around it. A river of life will flow out of Jerusalem – to east and to the west – turning the Dead Sea into a living sea, teeming with fish. Trees will grow on both banks, with fruit to eat month after month, and whose leaves bring healing to the nations.

8. All the nations of the earth will come up to Jerusalem to worship God and his Messiah and to celebrate the Feast of Tabernacles (*Succoth*). If they do not come up, they will receive no rain.

9. After the 1,000 years of righteous rule, Satan, who has been bound all this time, will be loosed to once again deceive the nations of the world and lead them in

a final attack on Jerusalem. Fire will come down from heaven and destroy them.

10. The earth and the heavens will melt away and disappear. The rest of the dead will be raised and judged before the great white throne of God. The beast, the false prophet, and all those whose names are not found in the Book of Life, will be cast into the lake of fire.

11. A new heaven and a new earth will be created by God and the '*New Jerusalem*' will come down from heaven and appear on the new earth, where God will dwell with his people for ever. And there will be no more death!

13 – Facing the Beast

So, the really good news is that Jesus is coming back to establish his reign on the earth and we will reign with him. The not so good news is that if we live long enough we may well come face to face with this dictator, the beast. Yeshua warned us that we would suffer persecution for his name. The scriptures give us plenty of information on his actions against God's people – they also describe how we should respond to his attacks and it is very important that we should learn from these and prepare our hearts accordingly.

Let's look at his attack on us first. He is empowered directly by Satan, so he carries that hatred that Satan has for all of God's people:

> **Revelation 12:1** A great sign appeared in heaven: <u>a woman clothed with the sun, with the moon under her feet and a crown of twelve stars on her head</u>. 2 She was pregnant and cried out in pain as she was about to give birth. 3 Then another sign appeared in heaven: an enormous red dragon with seven heads and ten horns and seven crowns on its heads. 4 Its tail swept a third of the stars out of the sky and flung them to the earth. <u>The dragon stood in front of the woman who was about to give birth, so that it might devour her child the moment he was born</u>. 5 She gave birth to a son, a male child, who 'will rule all the nations with an iron sceptre.' And her child was snatched up to God and to his throne. 6 <u>The woman fled into the wilderness to a place prepared for her</u> by God, <u>where she might be taken care of</u> for 1,260 days.
>
> 11 <u>They triumphed over him by the blood of the Lamb and by the word of their testimony; they did not love their lives so much as to shrink from death</u>.
>
> 13 When the dragon saw that he had been hurled to the earth, <u>he pursued the woman who had given birth to the male child</u>. 14 <u>The woman was given the two wings of a great eagle, so that she might fly to the place prepared for her in the</u>

wilderness, where she would be taken care of for a time, times and half a time, out of the snake's reach. 15 Then from his mouth the snake spewed water like a river, to overtake the woman and sweep her away with the torrent. 16 But the earth helped the woman by opening its mouth and swallowing the river that the dragon had spewed out of his mouth. 17 Then the dragon was enraged at the woman and went off to wage war against the rest of her offspring – those who keep God's commands and hold fast their testimony about Jesus.

First of all who is this woman? Her son *'will rule all the nations with an iron sceptre'* so we are talking about Jesus here. Jesus was birthed by Mary, but the woman described here is not Mary, but the nation of Israel. Some would identify the woman as the church, but that is not quite accurate, because the scripture tells us that we – the church – have been *'grafted in'* to the *'olive root'*, which is Israel:

> **Romans 11:16** If the part of the dough offered as firstfruits is holy, then the whole batch is holy; if the root is holy, so are the branches. 17 If some of the branches have been broken off, and you, though a wild olive shoot, have been grafted in among the others and now share in the nourishing sap from the olive root, 18 do not consider yourself to be superior to those other branches. If you do, consider this: you do not support the root, but the root supports you. 19 You will say then, 'Branches were broken off so that I could be grafted in.' 20 Granted. But they were broken off because of unbelief, and you stand by faith. Do not be arrogant, but tremble. 21 For if God did not spare the natural branches, he will not spare you either.

The church does not support Israel, the root – Israel – supports the branches – which we are. Paul amplifies this in his letter to the Ephesians:

> **Ephesians 2:11** Therefore, remember that formerly you who are Gentiles by birth and called 'uncircumcised' by those who call themselves 'the circumcision' (which is done in the body by human hands) – 12 remember that at that time you were separate from Christ, excluded from citizenship in Israel and foreigners to the covenants of the promise, without hope and without God in the world. 13 But now in Christ Jesus you who once were far away have been brought near by the blood of Christ.

Chapter 13 – Facing the Beast

19 <u>Consequently, you are no longer foreigners and strangers, but fellow citizens with God's people and also members of his household</u>, 20 built on the foundation of the apostles and prophets, with Christ Jesus himself as the chief cornerstone.

What is Paul saying? At one time we were *'excluded from citizenship in Israel'* and therefore we were separated from the promises of God, ***'but now'***, says Paul, *'<u>you</u> who once were far away <u>have been brought near</u> by the blood of Christ.'* The church has not replaced Israel – the church has been grafted into Israel! <u>We</u> have been *'grafted in.'*

'Consequently, you are no longer foreigners and strangers, but fellow citizens with God's people and also members of his household.' (**Ephesians 2:19**) See what Paul is telling us? We are no longer Gentiles, but a part of Israel, and as a result of our new *'citizenship in Israel'* we have become heirs to God's promises to Israel. That is why believers should have a strong connection with – and love for – Israel.

Here is the transformation that has taken place for Gentiles who come into a personal relationship with Yeshua, the Jewish Messiah – at that time you were:

- separate from Christ,
- excluded from citizenship in Israel
- foreigners to the covenants of the promise

but <u>now</u>:

- you have been brought near by the blood of Christ
- you are no longer foreigners and strangers
- you are fellow citizens with God's people
- you are members of his household

We are now a part of Israel! How does this affect the church? It means we are constrained by God to love and honour his people, Israel. He has a final plan for them, which includes salvation, mourning for their blindness in not recognising their messiah and deliverance from Satan's plan to destroy her:

Romans 11:24 After all, if you were cut out of an olive tree that is wild by nature, and contrary to nature were grafted into a cultivated olive tree, <u>how much more readily will these</u>, the natural branches, <u>be grafted into their own olive tree!</u>

25 I do not want you to be ignorant of this mystery, brothers and sisters, so that you may not be conceited: Israel has experienced a hardening <u>in part until the full number of the Gentiles has come in</u>, 26 and in this way <u>all Israel will be saved</u>.

There is a time coming when *'all Israel will be saved'*, when *'they will look on me, the one they have pierced, and they will mourn.'* The whole expanded nation of Israel will mourn and repent:

Zechariah 12:10 'And I will pour out on the house of David and the inhabitants of Jerusalem a spirit of grace and supplication. <u>They will look on me, the one they have pierced, and they will mourn for him as one mourns for an only child</u>, and grieve bitterly for him as one grieves for a firstborn son. 11 On that day the weeping in Jerusalem will be as great as the weeping of Hadad Rimmon in the plain of Megiddo. 12 <u>The land will mourn</u>, each clan by itself, with their wives by themselves: the clan of the house of David and their wives, the clan of the house of Nathan and their wives, 13 the clan of the house of Levi and their wives, the clan of Shimei and their wives, 14 and all the rest of the clans and their wives.

YHWH says, *'they will look on me, the one they have pierced.'*

Looking again at the woman of Revelation 12 (Israel) we see that she will be *'given the two wings of a great eagle, so that she might fly to the place prepared for her in the wilderness, where she would be taken care of for <u>a time, times and half a time</u>, out of the snake's reach.'*

God has a place prepared for Israel to be kept safe for the 3½ years of this persecution. *'Then the dragon [Satan] was enraged at the woman [Israel] and went off to wage war against the rest of her offspring [the church] – those who keep God's commands and hold fast their testimony about Jesus.'*

Yeshua warned his disciples to flee Jerusalem when they see Daniel's prophecy come to pass – the *'abomination of Desolation'*. This is when many people in Israel will be delivered and kept safe for the 3½ years of the *'great tribulation'* – i.e. *'Jacob's trouble'*.

'Then the dragon was enraged at the woman and <u>went off to wage war against the rest of her offspring – those who</u>

Chapter 13 – Facing the Beast

keep God's commands and <u>hold fast their testimony about Jesus.</u>' (**Revelation 12:17**) These people are believers in Yeshua – Christians. Unable to prevail against the majority of Israel, Satan – the great dragon – aided by his offspring, the antichrist, will persecute the church around the world.

Is this the wrath of God? No, it is the wrath of Satan against God's people. Yeshua foretold it:

> **Matthew 24:9** 'Then <u>you will be handed over to be persecuted and put to death, and you will be hated by all nations because of me. 10 At that time many will turn away from the faith and will betray and hate each other, 11 and many false prophets will appear and deceive many people. 12 Because of the increase of wickedness, the love of most will grow cold, 13 but the one who stands firm to the end will be saved</u>. 14 And this gospel of the kingdom will be preached in the whole world as a testimony to all nations, and then the end will come.
>
> 15 '<u>So when you see standing in the holy place "the abomination that causes desolation,"</u> spoken of through the prophet Daniel – let the reader understand – 16 <u>then</u> let those who are in Judea <u>flee to the mountains</u>. 17 Let no one on the housetop go down to take anything out of the house. 18 Let no one in the field go back to get their cloak. 19 How dreadful it will be in those days for pregnant women and nursing mothers! 20 <u>Pray that your flight will not take place in winter</u> or on the Sabbath. 21 <u>For then there will be great distress, unequalled from the beginning of the world until now</u> – and never to be equalled again.
>
> 22 'If those days had not been cut short, no one would survive, but for the sake of the elect those days will be shortened. 23 At that time if anyone says to you, "Look, here is the Messiah!" or, "There he is!" do not believe it. 24 For false messiahs and false prophets will appear and perform great signs and wonders to deceive, if possible, even the elect. 25 See, I have told you in advance.
>
> 26 'So if anyone tells you, "There he is, out in the desert," do not go out; or, "Here he is, in the inner rooms," do not believe it. 27 For as lightning that comes from the east is visible even in the west, so will be the coming of the Son of Man. 28 Wherever there is a carcass, there the vultures will gather.

'Wherever there is a carcase' – in other words, something stinks! And what stinks is the *'many'* people who will turn away from the faith and believe a lie – the lie of a false messiah. Jesus says, *'Do not believe it.'* and *'See, I have told you in advance.'* Is his warning to be disregarded?

Jesus says the people of Jerusalem and Judaea are to 'flee to the mountains' – he adds, *'pray that your flight will not be in winter.'* Revelation 12 states that the woman [Israel] will fly *to the place prepared for her in the wilderness'* – *'flee, flight, fly'* – there is a real sense of urgency in those words:

> **Daniel 11:32** With flattery he will corrupt those who have violated the covenant, but the people who know their God will firmly resist him. 33 'Those who are wise will instruct many, though for a time they will fall by the sword or be burned or captured or plundered. 34 When they fall, they will receive a little help, and many who are not sincere will join them. 35 Some of the wise will stumble, so that they may be refined, purified and made spotless until the time of the end, for it will still come at the appointed time.

What is God's purpose here? Daniel states it clearly, *'That we may be refined, purified and made spotless.'* Paul says the same thing, *'to present her to himself as a radiant church, without stain or wrinkle or any other blemish, but holy and blameless.'*

So, if we are living in Israel and heed Yeshua's warning to flee Jerusalem in time – i.e. when the abomination is set up in the temple – then many living in Israel will escape to the mountains/wilderness and be protected there for the 3½ years of 'Jacob's Trouble' – the *'great tribulation.'*

Where is this place in the wilderness/mountains? Many believe Jesus was referring to Petra, in present-day Jordan – are they correct?

> **Daniel 11:41** He will also invade the Beautiful Land. Many countries will fall, but Edom, Moab and the leaders of Ammon will be delivered from his hand.

The *'king of the north'* – i.e. the antichrist – *'will invade the beautiful land ... but Edom, Moab and the leaders of Ammon will be delivered from his hand.'* The beast will not

Chapter 13 – Facing the Beast

succeed in invading the former kingdom of Jordan – now a part of greater Israel – which is composed of mountains and could easily be described as wilderness.

But if we are not living in Israel then the full wrath of Satan and the beast will be vented *'against the rest of her* [the woman's] *offspring – those who keep God's commands and hold fast their testimony about Jesus.'* (**Matthew 12:17**)

How can we prepare for this? We are given encouragement each time these events are described to us:

> **Daniel 11:32** With flattery he will corrupt those who have violated the covenant, <u>but the people who know their God will firmly resist him</u>. 33 "<u>Those who are wise will instruct many</u>, though for a time they will fall by the sword or be burned or captured or plundered. 34 When they fall, <u>they will receive a little help</u>, and many who are not sincere will join them. 35 Some of the wise will stumble, so that they may be refined, purified and made spotless <u>until the time of the end, for it will still come</u> at the appointed time.

> **Daniel 12:3** Those who are wise will shine like the brightness of the heavens, and those who lead many to righteousness, like the stars for ever and ever.

So, we need to focus on becoming *'people who know their God,'* who are wise and can *'instruct many'* – *'lead many to righteousness.'* How can we instruct anyone if we do not study and seek God to know what he says about these things?

We have examples of this in many parts of the world today. Persecution of believers in Yeshua is happening all over the world as you read this. Just because we only experience comparatively mild opposition in the west – at present – does not mean we won't experience the same thing. Jesus said we will be *'hated by <u>all nations</u>'* (**Matthew 24:9**) – so our turn is surely coming!

Jesus follows that statement by telling us that many will not be able to withstand this, but will *'turn away'* from him:

> **Matthew 24:9** 'Then <u>you will be handed over to be persecuted and put to death, and you will be hated by all nations because of me. 10 At that time many will turn away from the faith and will betray and hate each other,</u> 11 and

many false prophets will appear and deceive many people. 12 <u>Because of the increase of wickedness, the love of most will grow cold, 13 but the one who stands firm to the end will be saved</u>. 14 And <u>this gospel of the kingdom will be preached in the whole world as a testimony to all nations, and then the end will come</u>.

The *'end will come'*, but Yeshua expects us to *'stand firm to the end.'* How can we do this?

2 Peter 3:9 The Lord is not slow in keeping his promise, as some understand slowness. Instead he is patient with you, <u>not wanting anyone to perish</u>, but everyone to come to repentance.

10 But the day of the Lord will come like a thief. The heavens will disappear with a roar; the elements will be destroyed by fire, and the earth and everything done in it will be laid bare.

11 Since everything will be destroyed in this way, <u>what kind of people ought you to be? You ought to live holy and godly lives 12 as you look forward to the day of God and speed its coming</u>. That day will bring about the destruction of the heavens by fire, and the elements will melt in the heat. 13 But in keeping with his promise we are looking forward to a new heaven and a new earth, where righteousness dwells.

14 So then, dear friends, since you are looking forward to this, <u>make every effort to be found spotless, blameless and at peace with him</u>. 15 Bear in mind that our Lord's patience means salvation, just as our dear brother Paul also wrote you with the wisdom that God gave him. 16 He writes the same way in all his letters, speaking in them of these matters. His letters contain some things that are hard to understand, which ignorant and unstable people distort, <u>as they do the other Scriptures</u>, to their own destruction.

17 Therefore, dear friends, <u>since you have been forewarned, be on your guard so that you may not be carried away by the error of the lawless and fall from your secure position. 18 But grow in the grace and knowledge of our Lord and Saviour Jesus Christ</u>.

Peter asks, *'What kind of people ought you to be?'* (**v. 11**) then answers his own question, *'You ought to live holy and godly lives as you look forward to the day of God <u>and speed its coming</u>.'* So we can speed up the day when Jesus returns

Chapter 13 – Facing the Beast

– by living holy and godly lives! That is an incentive right there. Imagine the Lord telling us one day that our living actually brought his return more quickly!

We are to *'make every effort to be found spotless, blameless and at peace with him.'* We are to, *'be on [our] guard so that [we] may not be carried away by the error of the lawless and fall from [our] secure position.* And finally, we are to, *'grow in the grace and knowledge of our Lord and Saviour Jesus Christ.'*

To sum up, Peter tells us to:

• *live holy and godly lives as you look forward to the day of God*

• *make every effort to be found spotless, blameless and at peace with him*

• *be on your guard so that you may not be carried away by the error of the lawless and fall from your secure position*

• *grow in the grace and knowledge of our Lord and Saviour Jesus Christ*

Peter has some more timely advice for us in his first letter:

1 Peter 4:7 <u>The end of all things is near. Therefore be alert and of sober mind so that you may pray</u>. 8 Above all, <u>love each other deeply, because love covers over a multitude of sins</u>. 9 <u>Offer hospitality to one another without grumbling</u>. 10 Each of you should use whatever gift you have received to <u>serve others, as faithful stewards of God's grace</u> in its various forms. 11 If anyone speaks, they should do so as one who speaks the very words of God. If anyone serves, they should do so with the strength God provides, so that in all things God may be praised through Jesus Christ.

Because the *'end of all things is near'* we should respond by being alert (there is that word again!), being sober – not dour, or aloof, but not caught up in the ways of the world, either – and praying. Above all, demonstrating his love for one another, serving one another with whatever abilities God has given us – faithful stewards.

12 Dear friends, <u>do not be surprised at the fiery ordeal that has come on you to test you, as though something strange were</u>

happening to you. 13 But rejoice inasmuch as you participate in the sufferings of Christ, so that you may be over-joyed when his glory is revealed. 14 <u>If you are insulted because of the name of Christ, you are blessed</u>, for the Spirit of glory and of God rests on you. 15 <u>If you suffer</u>, it should not be as a murderer or thief or any other kind of criminal, or even as a meddler. 16 However, if you <u>suffer as a Christian, do not be ashamed, but praise God that you bear that name</u>. 17 For it is time for judgment to begin with God's household; and if it begins with us, what will the outcome be for those who do not obey the gospel of God? 18 And, 'If it is hard for the righteous to be saved, what will become of the ungodly and the sinner?'

19 So then, <u>those who suffer according to God's will should commit themselves to their faithful Creator and continue to do good</u>.

Well, there goes that idea we had that *'God wouldn't want us to suffer, would he?'* – sorry, it's not scriptural! Peter says, *'those who suffer according to God's will.'* Peter makes it perfectly clear that persecution should not be regarded as abnormal, *'as though something strange were happening to you.'* No, it is to be expected!

Most of the Christian church – except in the west – are already experiencing persecution, some of it quite extreme. Wake up, people! Don't live any longer in your fantasy land!

I went through a time of mild persecution some years ago, when my daughters were young and were still living at home. When I asked those I was in fellowship with for prayer support some of them questioned me as to whether I had done some-thing wrong, or suggested that maybe God was telling me we should move out of that area.

Neither of these was the correct response. Several of them had no concept that persecution was normal, that it was possibly a sign that we might have been doing something right – i.e. praying for our area and prayer-walking it, meeting there as a cell group. I remember one of those people suggesting that the only way to respond was to demonstrate Jesus' love to our neighbours – we felt that was a word from God.

Chapter 13 – Facing the Beast

The result of the prayer, etc., was that a number of people were healed and made a commitment to the Lord. Our small cell group grew and multiplied and those who had been giving us grief – mainly drug dealers and members of paramilitary groups – were either spoken to by the Lord, or they moved away out of the area entirely.

The whole atmosphere in our area changed and my wife and I – who had previously been threatened that we would be forced to move out, that more of our windows would be broken, even that our house would be burnt down – are still living in that same house in peace and quiet!

1 Peter 5:5 In the same way, you who are younger, submit yourselves to your elders. <u>All of you, clothe yourselves with humility towards one another,</u> because, 'God opposes the proud but shows favour to the humble.' 6 Humble yourselves, therefore, under God's mighty hand, that he may lift you up in due time. 7 Cast all your anxiety on him because he cares for you.

8 <u>Be alert and of sober mind</u>. Your enemy the devil prowls around like a roaring lion looking for someone to devour. 9 <u>Resist him, standing firm in the faith</u>, because <u>you know that the family of believers throughout the world is under-going the same kind of sufferings</u>.

Again Peter tells us to *'be alert and of sober mind.'* What does he mean? That we should go around with long faces, spouting doom and gloom all of the time? Not at all! But I do think he means us to take the words of the Hebrew prophets seriously, to be fully aware of the things that are coming upon the world and to be prepared by reaching out to our communities, making friendships, making disciples, demonstrating his love for all men.

Jesus himself also warned us in three parables (**Matthew 25**) as to how we should prepare for his coming. The chapter is quite long so I'll take it one parable at a time:

Matthew 25:1 '<u>At that time</u> the kingdom of heaven will be like ten virgins who took their lamps and went out to meet the bridegroom. 2 <u>Five of them were foolish and five were wise</u>. 3 <u>The foolish ones took their lamps but did not take any oil with them</u>. 4 The wise ones, however, took oil in jars along with their lamps. 5 The bridegroom was a long time in coming, and they all became drowsy and fell asleep.

6 'At midnight the cry rang out: "Here's the bridegroom! Come out to meet him!" 7 'Then all the virgins woke up and trimmed their lamps. 8 The foolish ones said to the wise, "Give us some of your oil; our lamps are going out." 9 '"No," they replied, "there may not be enough for both us and you. Instead, go to those who sell oil and buy some for yourselves." 10 'But while they were on their way to buy the oil, the bridegroom arrived. The virgins who were ready went in with him to the wedding banquet. And the door was shut. 11 'Later the others also came. "Lord, Lord," they said, "open the door for us!" 12 'But he replied, "Truly I tell you, I don't know you." 13 '<u>Therefore keep watch, because you do not know the day or the hour</u>.

What was Yeshua's point in this parable? The five wise girls had brought jars of oil with their lamps – so they were prepared for the long haul. The foolish ones went out, but had not made any serious preparations. When the bridegroom delayed, their lamps began to run out of oil.

We need to make proper preparation for a time of tribulation now – not *'wait to see how it all pans out!'* It may well be too late by then! We don't want to be among those who – deceived by the false promise of a *'secret rapture'* – are so let down when it fails to happen that they *'turn away from the faith'* – as Jesus foretold that *'many'* would do. That is why he began his response by saying, *'Watch out that no one deceives you.'*

So, should we be building a cabin way out in the woods and laying in stores, etc.? I don't think that is how Jesus is meaning us to prepare. He is the God of the supernatural, he is more than able to provide for all of our needs, but we need to be willing to take risks for his sake and that of the gospel.

Jesus continued with the parable of the bags of gold:

Matthew 25:14 'Again, it will be like a man going on a journey, who called his servants and entrusted his wealth to them. 15 To one he gave five bags of gold, to another two bags, and to another one bag, each according to his ability.

Chapter 13 – Facing the Beast

Then he went on his journey. 16 The man who had received five bags of gold went at once and put his money to work and gained five bags more. 17 So also, the one with two bags of gold gained two more. 18 But the man who had received one bag went off, dug a hole in the ground and hid his master's money.

19 'After a long time the master of those servants returned and settled accounts with them. 20 The man who had received five bags of gold brought the other five. "Master," he said, "you entrusted me with five bags of gold. See, I have gained five more." 21 'His master replied, "Well done, good and faithful servant! You have been faithful with a few things; I will put you in charge of many things. Come and share your master's happiness!"

22 'The man with two bags of gold also came. "Master," he said, "you entrusted me with two bags of gold: see, I have gained two more." 23 'His master replied, "Well done, good and faithful servant! You have been faithful with a few things; I will put you in charge of many things. Come and share your master's happiness!"

24 'Then the man who had received one bag of gold came. "Master," he said, "I knew that you are a hard man, harvesting where you have not sown and gathering where you have not scattered seed. 25 So I was afraid and went out and hid your gold in the ground. See, here is what belongs to you." 26 'His master replied, "You wicked, lazy servant! So you knew that I harvest where I have not sown and gather where I have not scattered seed? 27 Well then, you should have put my money on deposit with the bankers, so that when I returned I would have received it back with interest. 28 "'So take the bag of gold from him and give it to the one who has ten bags. 29 For whoever has will be given more, and they will have an abundance. Whoever does not have, even what they have will be taken from them. 30 And throw that worthless servant outside, into the darkness, where there will be weeping and gnashing of teeth."

The servants with five bags and two bags took some immediate action – they went out with what they had. They didn't wait to *'see how things would pan out!'* They started to use what the master had given them – this is a warning to many so-called believers who do little more than sit in church pews and absorb, week after week.

Yeshua has called us firstly to <u>be</u> disciples, secondly to go out and <u>make</u> disciples. What was the third servant's mistake – he did nothing with what he had been given. He didn't understand that his master wanted him to take risks with what he had. Instead he tried to keep it safe by burying it. This is <u>not</u> Jesus' plan for us!

I recently watched the documentary film, *'Sheep Among Wolves'* – the story of the world's fastest growing church, in Iran. Although they have no buildings, money or visible leadership, and their outreach is mainly achieved by women – women in burkas, who are very liable to be raped for their stand for Yeshua – they have established a vibrant Disciple Making Movement (DMM), which has now come to the attention of the highest leaders in the Islamic Republic.

One American, who has met many of the members of this movement, commented on their strategy, *'Jesus didn't tell us to go out and plant churches, <u>he told us to go and make disciples</u>.'* Obviously, if we make disciples in a new area a church will result, but the emphasis is subtly different – anyone can make disciples, even someone relatively new in the things of God.

Yeshua's third parable was about the sheep and the goats:

> 31 'When the Son of Man comes in his glory, and all the angels with him, he will sit on his glorious throne. 32 All the nations will be gathered before him, and he will separate the people one from another as a shepherd separates the sheep from the goats. 33 He will put the sheep on his right and the goats on his left.
>
> 34 'Then the King will say to those on his right, "<u>Come, you who are blessed by my Father; take your inheritance</u>, the kingdom prepared for you since the creation of the world. 35 For I was hungry and you gave me something to eat, I was thirsty and you gave me something to drink, I was a stranger and you invited me in, 36 I needed clothes and you clothed me, I was ill and you looked after me, I was in prison and you came to visit me."
>
> 37 'Then the righteous will answer him, "Lord, when did we see you hungry and feed you, or thirsty and give you some-

Chapter 13 – Facing the Beast

thing to drink? 38 When did we see you a stranger and invite you in, or needing clothes and clothe you? 39 When did we see you ill or in prison and go to visit you?"

40 'The King will reply, "Truly I tell you, whatever you did for one of the least of these brothers and sisters of mine, you did for me." 41 'Then he will say to those on his left, "<u>Depart from me, you who are cursed</u>, into the eternal fire prepared for the devil and his angels. 42 For I was hungry and you gave me nothing to eat, I was thirsty and you gave me nothing to drink, 43 I was a stranger and you did not invite me in, I needed clothes and you did not clothe me, I was ill and in prison and you did not look after me."

44 'They also will answer, "Lord, when did we see you hungry or thirsty or a stranger or needing clothes or ill or in prison, and did not help you?" 45 'He will reply, "Truly I tell you, <u>whatever you did not do</u> for one of the least of these, <u>you did not do for me</u>." 46 'Then they will go away to eternal punishment, but the righteous to eternal life.'

Again, this does not require years of bible college training, this is something that every one of us can do – see the need and take action, as if we were serving Yeshua himself.

Remember what Daniel said? '<u>The people who know their God will firmly resist him. 'Those who are wise will instruct many</u>, though for a time they will fall by the sword or be burned or captured or plundered. When they fall, they will receive a little help ... so that they may be refined, purified and made spotless, until the time of the end.' (**Daniel 11:32-35**)

Resist who? The antichrist! We have a mission to fulfil – to reach every tribe, people, tongue and nation with the good news:

Matthew 24:12 Because of the increase of wickedness, the love of most will grow cold, 13 but <u>the one who stands firm to the end will be saved</u>. 14 And <u>this gospel of the kingdom will be preached in the whole world as a testimony to all nations, and then the end will come.</u>

22 If those days had not been cut short, no-one would survive, but for the sake of the elect <u>those days will be shortened</u>.

2 Peter 3:11 What kind of people ought you to be? You ought to live holy and godly lives 12 as you look forward to the day of God and speed its coming.

So, how should we face the beast? We must prepare our hearts to endure persecution to the end and meantime we reach out with all of our ability in order to *'instruct many'* and to *'reach the whole world with the gospel of the kingdom ... and then* (says Yeshua] *the end will come!'* Hallelujah!

Then *'he will send his angels with a loud trumpet call, and they will gather his elect from the four winds, from one end of the heavens to the other.'* (**Matthew 24:31**)

Titus 2:11 For the grace of God has appeared that offers salvation to all people. 12 It teaches us to say 'No' to ungodliness and worldly passions, and to live self-controlled, upright and godly lives in this present age, 13 while we wait for the blessed hope – the appearing of the glory of our great God and Saviour, Jesus Christ, 14 who gave himself for us to redeem us from all wickedness and to purify for himself a people that are his very own, eager to do what is good.

1 Thessalonians 4:16 For the Lord himself will come down from heaven, with a loud command, with the voice of the archangel and with the trumpet call of God, and the dead in Christ will rise first. 17 After that, we who are still alive and are left will be caught up together with them in the clouds to meet the Lord in the air. And so we will be with the Lord for ever. 18 Therefore encourage one another with these words.

Be encouraged!

Facing the Beast – a summary:

1. Jesus is surely coming back to earth to reign over it! This is good news and *'the blessed hope!'* (**Titus 2:13**)

2. The less comforting news is that we may live to see *'man of lawlessness',* the beast, face to face. (**2 Thessalonians 2:3**)

3. We (the church) have been *'grafted in'* to the olive root – Israel, the woman of **Revelation 12**.

4. The church has not replaced Israel in God's plan, rather we have received, *'citizenship in Israel,'* through the blood of the Messiah.

5. There is a time coming when *'all Israel will be saved'* (**Romans 11:26**), when *'they will look on me, the one they have pierced, and they will mourn.'* (**Zechariah 12:10**)

6. Yeshua warned the people of Judah and Jerusalem to *'flee to the mountains'* when they see the *'abomination of desolation'* being set up in the Temple – *'flee, flight, fly.'*

7. **Revelation 12** states that the woman will be taken care of in the wilderness for 3½ years. Where? It seems that former Jordan *'will be delivered from* [the beast's] *hand.'* (**Daniel 11:41**)

8. *'Then the dragon … went off to wage war against the rest of her offspring – those who … hold fast their testimony about Jesus.'* We believers are going to experience great persecution.

9. This is NOT the wrath of God, but the wrath of Satan and his antichrist. Jesus warned us that we would be *'hated by all nations.'* (**Matthew 24:9**)

10. *'The people who know their God will firmly resist him. "Those who are wise will instruct many., though for a time they will fall by the sword or be burned or captured or plundered.'* (**Daniel 11:32**)

11. Persecution of believers in Yeshua is happening all over the world right now – Jesus said we will be *'hated by <u>all nations</u>'* (**Matthew 24:9**)

12. Because of persecution – and also probably because of the *'secret rapture'* deception and the inevitable disappointment when that proves false – *'many will turn away from the faith.'* (**Matthew 24:9-13**)

13. *'The <u>one who stands firm to the end will be saved</u>. And this gospel of the kingdom will be preached in the whole world ... and <u>then the end will come</u>.'* (**Matthew 24:13,14**)

14. Peter says we *'ought to live holy and godly lives as you look forward to the day of God and speed its coming.'* (**2 Peter 3:11,12**)

15. He also says to *'be alert and of sober mind so that you may pray ... above all, love.'* (**1 Peter 4:7.8**)

16. We are *'not* [to] *be surprised'* at persecution *'as though something strange were happening to you.'* (**v.12**)

17. *'Those who <u>suffer according to God's will.</u>'* (**v.19**) Persecution is to be expected!

18. So, we are to *'resist* [Satan], *standing firm in the faith, because you know that the family of believers throughout the world is undergoing the same kind of sufferings.'* (**1 Peter 5:9**)

19. Jesus also told us to be prepared – like the girls who took extra oil for their lamps. (**Matthew 25:4**) – not by hiding from the world, but by reaching out in love to spread the gospel to every nation. (**Matthew 24:14**)

20. Two of the servants in Jesus' parable took the risk (**Matthew 25:14-30**) and put their master's money to work so that it produced fruit – the third wouldn't take the risk and was condemned by his master. We need to take risks of faith to reach the world around us with the good news.

21. Jesus called us – not to plant churches, which might require a lot of expertise – but to make disciples, (**Matthew 28:19**) which all of us are capable of doing.

22. Jesus taught us that as we did it to the least of his brothers, we did it to him – we can meet the needs of the hungry, the thirsty, the lonely, the prisoner (**Matthew 25:31-46**) – demonstrating the love of Christ is not rocket science!

Chapter 13 – Facing the Beast

23. How should we face the beast? Prepare our hearts to endure persecution to the end and meantime reach out with all of our ability, in order to *'instruct many'* and to *'reach the whole world with the gospel of the kingdom.'*

24. Then *'he will send his angels ... and they will gather his elect from ... one end of the heavens to the other.'* (**Matthew 24:31**)

25. *'We wait for the blessed hope – the appearing of ... Jesus,'* (**Titus 2:1**) then *'we who are still alive and are left will be caught up ... in the clouds to meet the Lord in the air. And so we will be with the Lord for ever.'* (**1 Thessalonians 4:17**)

26. *'Therefore encourage one another with these words.'* (**v.18**) – so be encouraged!

Bibliography

The Biblical Hebrew Origin of the Japanese People
Joseph Eidelberg

Discovered: Noah's Ark*
Ron Wyatt

DNA and Tradition:
The Genetic Link to the Ancient Hebrews*
Rabbi Yaakov Kleiman

The Exodus Case
Dr. Lennart Möller

Jews in Places You Never Thought Of*
by Karen Primack

Scattered Among the Nations*
Bryan Schwartz

The Islamic Antichrist – The Shocking Truth about the Real Nature of the Beast
Joel Richardson

* Recommended

Appendix
Note on translations

We have used the **New International Version** (NIV) throughout this book. It is a reasonably accurate English translation, whilst also being easy to read. In some passages another translation may have been more helpful and we recommend comparing translations of these prophetic writings.

Name of God, etc.

We also had to make a decision regarding the words 'God' and 'Lord'. Initially, we followed the traditional rabbinical Judaism route of writing God as G-d and LORD as L-RD, however, too many people found this confusing and even annoying, so we have kept the names as they are in the NIV translation. There is no intention to cause any offence to Rabbinical Jews.

Following on from this, another important point is that the Hebrew tetragrammaton, יהוה ('YHWH' in English), is normally replaced in modern Jewish* use with the Hebrew word, *'Adonai',* meaning Lord. Christian translators have generally decided to follow this tradition and substitute 'LORD' (in capitals) for Yehovah, (sometimes spoken as Yahweh).

As we are called to make known the name of YHWH it seems a great pity if neither the Jews, nor Christians, are prepared to use the actual name of God. The Hebrew scriptures (even in the New Testament) advocate that we make known the Name of God. His Name is *not* 'The Lord', 'Adonai' (Lord), or 'HaShem' (The Name), or 'Master' (baal, in Hebrew), but

---

* Many Karaite Jews DO use and pronounce the tetragrammaton, יהוה, for the Name of God.

'YHWH' (pronounced Yehowah, Yehovah, or sometimes, Yahweh).

Throughout this book I have used the english letters, YHWH, in place of the tetragrammaton, יהוה. I believe it is only right to properly honour the name of God by doing so.

About the author:

Raymond McCullough, from Co. Down, near Belfast, Northern Ireland, has been a professional writer since 1988, originally writing a regular series – plus other articles, reviews and reports – for several UK technical magazines.

From 1990-96 he edited and published the Irish magazine, *'Bread'* – releasing his first book, *'Ireland – now the good news!'* from this in 1995; co-edited by his wife, well-known fiction author Gerry McCullough. His articles have also been published in the *Irish Times*, Dublin, and the *Presbyterian Herald*, Belfast.

In 1993 he hosted a radio show, 'In tha Name a' Gawd!' on 96.7 BCR, in Belfast, which later developed into his current satellite radio show of music, news and faith-based interviews – broadcasting around the world on several satellite networks. From 1996, for seven years, he and Gerry led a cell-based Christian fellowship in the Belfast area.

Since then he's been involved in media of all kinds – from web design to podcasting, satellite and internet radio, plus documentary TV production – producing an album of Celtic & Hebrew worship music, *'Into Jerusalem,'* in 2005 and a Celtic pop-folk album, *'Different,'* in 2008.

Raymond has researched the subjects in *'The Whore and her Mother'* for about forty years, off and on, but the events of 9/11 brought a new focus to his research and a real sense of increasing urgency encouraged him to complete the book in just four months! He felt the subject was too interesting and dramatic to simply be confined to the fairly narrow, evangelical Christian world.

Since 2008, Raymond has produced and hosted *'Celtic Roots Radio'* – an *Apple* and *Google* podcast and web station (on *Shoutcast*) – listened to in over 100 countries. He also produces and hosts the *'In tha Name a' Gawd!'* testimony series and *Fresh Bread* – broadcasting each week on satellite. His *'Kingdom Come Trust'* website has hundreds of enthusiastic emails from satellite radio listeners in US, Canada, Australia and the Caribbean.

Raymond has two more bible prophecy books in this *Arrows* series entitled, *'Oh What Rapture!'* and *'Neighbours from Hell.'* The *Six Hours* series is fiction, but inspired by bible prophecy – *'In Six Hours …the world changed'* and *'In One Hour … Babylon will fall.'* The third book of the trilogy, *'In the Final Hour … the King will return'* is currently being written.

Raymond is also writing a follow-up to *'The Whore and her Mother'* entitled, *'What Kinda People?'* – expanding the contents of his last chapter (WHM) on how we should respond to these prophecies soon to be fulfilled; and is working on a book about Israel, called, *'The Chosen: Israelites, past, present and future'*. He is also currently editing a TV documentary, filmed mainly in Canada, about the relationship between Scottish and Irish immigrants and Native Americans – entitled, *'Broken Treaties.'*

More info at:

http://www.raymondmccullough.com
http://www.kingdomcome.org.uk

More fiction and non-fiction books by this author:

The Whore and her Mother
9/11, Babylon and the return of the king

Oh What Rapture!
Arrows bible prophecy series, book #1

Is a 'secret rapture' going to spare believers from tribulation to come?

Neighbours from Hell
Arrows bible prophecy series, book #2

Israel and the coming nuclear attempt to destroy her

Facing the Beast
Arrows bible prophecy series, book #3

The man they call the antichrist and our response to him

In Six Hours ... the world changed
Apocalyptic fiction thriller

In One Hour ... Babylon will fall
Apocalyptic fiction thriller – sequel

Ireland – now the good news!
The best of *'Bread'* – personal testimonies and church/fellowship profiles from around Ireland
Edited by *Raymond & Gerry McCullough*

A Wee Taste a' Craic
all the Irish craic from the *Celtic Roots Radio* shows, 2-25

Fiction from *Gerry McCullough*:

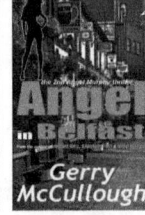

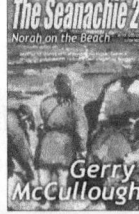

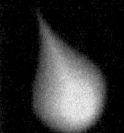

www.ingramcontent.com/pod-product-compliance
Lightning Source LLC
Chambersburg PA
CBHW061325040426
42444CB00011B/2786